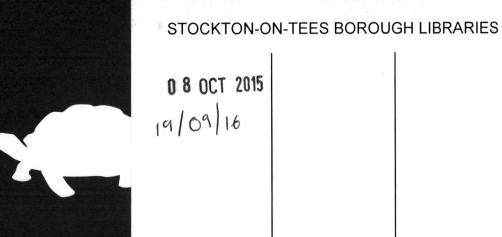

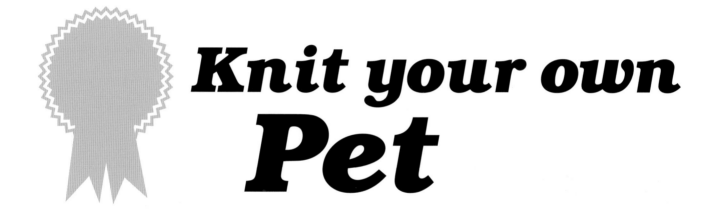

Knit your own
Pet

First published in the United Kingdom
in 2014 by
Collins & Brown
10 Southcombe Street
London W14 0RA

An imprint of Anova Books Company Ltd

Photography by Holly Jolliffe

ISBN 978-1-90844-941-2

A CIP catalogue for this book is available
from the British Library.

10 9 8 7 6 5 4 3 2 1

Printed by Toppan Leefung Ltd, China
Repro by Rival Colour Ltd, UK

This book can be ordered direct from the
publisher at www.anovabooks.com

For the pets:

Shadrach, Meshach and Abednego, the bantam hens
Caspar, the bearded dragon
Hajikucheek, the mynah bird
Starlight, the Shetland pony
Sticky, the stick insect
Hammy, Peace, Love, Justice, Beauty, the hamsters
Hengist and Horsa, the gerbils
Audrey, Max, Mika and Lulu, the rats
Geoffrey, Sally, Abigail and Gabriel, the goldfish

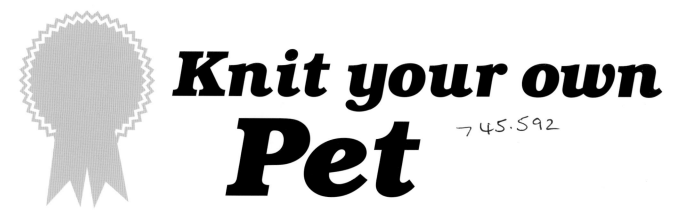

Knit your own
Pet

745.592

Sally Muir & Joanna Osborne

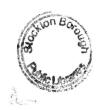

COLLINS & BROWN

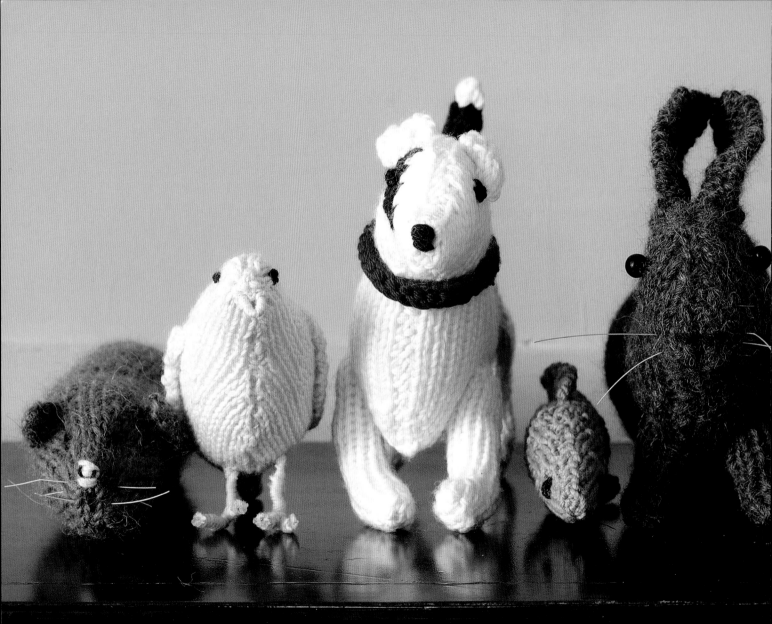

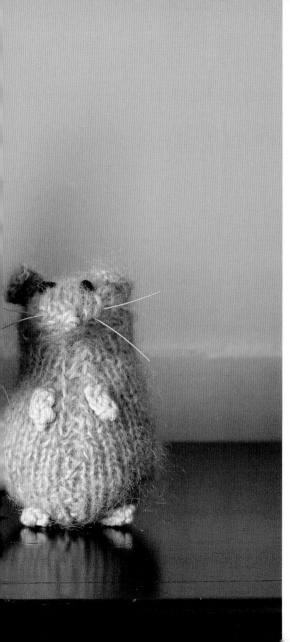

Contents

6 Introduction
8 How To Knit

14 Small And Furry
16 Hamster
20 Ferret
26 Mouse
30 Rabbit

36 Birds
38 Canary
42 Parrot

46 Four-Legged Friends
48 Simple Cat
54 Simple Dog
60 Shetland Pony
66 Guinea Pig

70 Reptiles And Fish
72 Axolotl
76 Bearded Dragon
80 Cornsnake
84 Goldfish
88 Tortoise

94 Index Of Pets
96 Resources
96 Acknowledgements

Introduction

There are very many reasons why you might want to knit yourself a pet: maybe you aren't allowed that ferret that you've always craved; your goldfish has moved on to the Great Goldfish Bowl in the Sky; there isn't any room for a pony in your house; your cat might take too much interest in a real mouse. The knitted pet avoids many of the problems of the real pet, giving you lovely woolly companionship with none of the drawbacks. The knitted pet is perfectly house-trained, never nips, will not escape and will never die, and you will also have the satisfaction of knowing that you made it yourself.

Knit Your Own Pet is a book for the beginner knitter. We have made our patterns simple so that they can be easily achieved. Some of our pets are quicker to knit and smaller than others and we have given each a rosette rating, from one to three, to help you decide where to start. It would be a good idea if you are a very new knitter to begin with a one-rosette pet, something very simple like the Mouse or Goldfish, which are small and quick to make and will give you a great sense of achievement. You can then move on to tackle something a little harder like the Cornsnake or Guinea Pig, which are also one-rosette pets and so still easy, but will take a little longer.

Then you can move onto the Simple Cat and Dog, which are larger and are two-rosette pets. Finally, when you have practised on all those, you can make the Shetland Pony and Ferret, which are the most complicated in the book and both three-rosette, but are still not very difficult.

You can change yarns to make your pets in different colours to ours, and if you use thicker yarn and bigger needles, you'll get a bigger pet. Bear in mind that if you want to give a pet to a small child, it's best not to give those that have to have pipecleaners, like the Canary: you can get by without using pipecleaners in most of the animals if you make sure to stuff the legs firmly.

We hope that you'll enjoy making the pets as much as we did.

Joanna and Sally

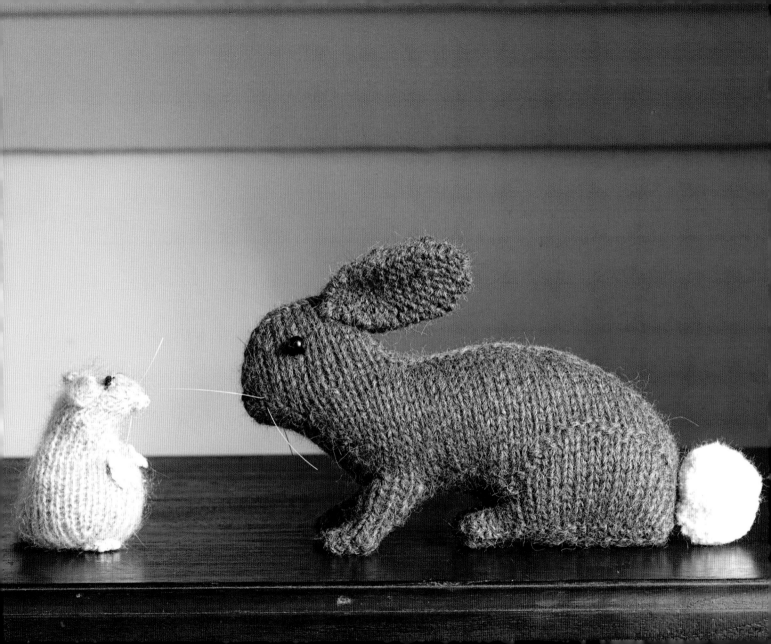

How To Knit

If you are a total beginner knitter, then we are quite envious, as a lot of pleasure awaits you as you learn to knit. You might find holding the needles and yarn a bit awkward at first, but practise just knitting rows with some spare yarn before you start on the simplest project in the book (we suggest the Mouse on page 26 or the Goldfish on page 84), and you'll soon get the hang of it.

To help you get started the basic knitting techniques are shown on the following pages; there are also lots of good video tutorials on the Web if you'd like to see knitting in action.

We have given each of our pets a rosette rating, from one to three, to help you decide where to start. It is a good idea for new knitters to begin with a one-rosette pet.

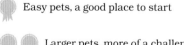 Easy pets, a good place to start

Larger pets, more of a challenge

The most complicated pets

Slip Knot

To cast on you need a slip knot, which will always count as the first cast-on stitch.

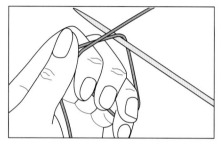

1 Hold the working (ball) end of the yarn in your right hand and wrap it around the fingers of your left hand. Put the tip of a knitting needle, held in your right hand, through the loop around your fingers.

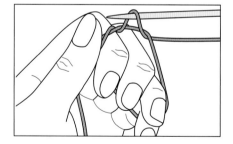

2 Wrap the working end of the yarn round the needle and pull the needle, and the yarn wrapped around it, through the loop around your left hand.

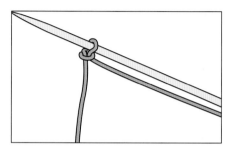

3 Keeping the yarn on the needle, slip the loop off your left hand. Pull gently on the ends of the yarn so that the loop tightens around the needle.

Holding The Needles And Yarn

Try this popular way of holding the knitting needles and the yarn.

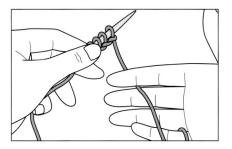

1 Hold the needle with the stitches on in your left hand. Wrap the yarn around the little finger of your right hand and then come up between your index and second fingers.

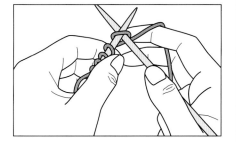

2 Hold the other needle in your right hand in the same way as you would hold a pencil. The right-hand index finger is going to control the tension of the yarn, so it is important to keep the yarn slightly taut around this finger.

Cable Cast On

The first step is to create the number of stitches needed on the needles.

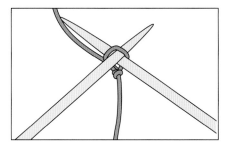

1 Make a slip knot about 10cm (4in) from the end of the yarn. Hold the needle with the slip knot in your left hand and the other needle in your right hand. Put the tip of the right-hand needle into the front of the stitch on the left-hand needle (remember that the slip knot is the first stitch). Bring the working yarn under and around the point of the right-hand needle.

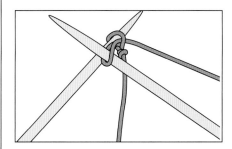

2 Pull the yarn taut so that it is wrapped around the tip of the right-hand needle. Bring the tip of the right-hand needle, and the loop of yarn wrapped around it, through the stitch and towards you.

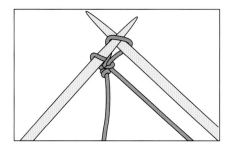

3 Slip the loop over the tip of the left-hand needle to make a new stitch on that needle. Take the right-hand needle out of the loop and pull the working end of the yarn to tighten the stitch.

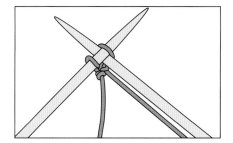

4 To cast on all the other stitches, put the tip of the right-hand needle between the last two stitches, instead of through the last one. Then repeat Seps 1–3 until you have the required number of stitches on the left-hand needle.

Knit Stitch

The first stitch to learn. This is very like casting on stitches.

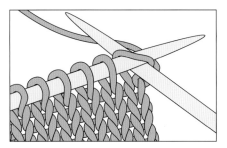

1 From front to back, insert the tip of the right-hand needle into the first stitch on the left-hand needle.Bring the yarn you are holding in your right hand under the tip of the right-hand needle.

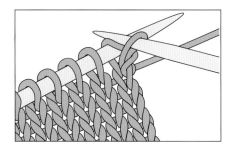

3 Bring the tip of the right-hand needle, and the loop of yarn wrapped around it, through the stitch on the left-hand needle to make a new stitch on the right-hand needle.

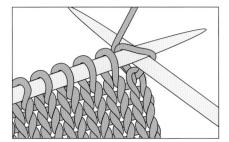

2 Wrap the yarn over the needle.

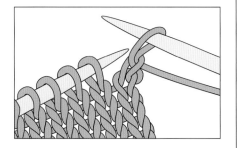

4 Slip the original stitch off the left-hand needle. The knitted stitch is now complete.

Purl Stitch

The only other knitting stitch to learn.

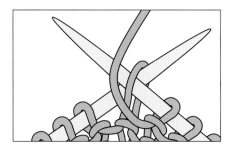

1 For purl stitch, the yarn is held at the front of the work, as shown. From back to front, put the tip of the right-hand needle into the first stitch on the left-hand needle. Bring the yarn forward and then take it over the tip of the right-hand needle.

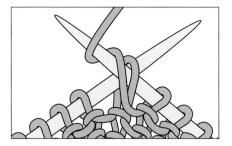

2 Wrap it around the tip of the needle.

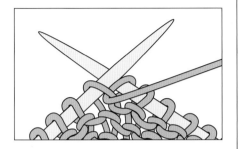

3 Bring the tip of the right-hand needle, and the loop of yarn wrapped around it, backwards through the stitch on the left-hand needle to make a new stitch on the right-hand needle.

Casting (Binding) Off

When you have finished knitting a piece, you need to stop the stitches unravelling.

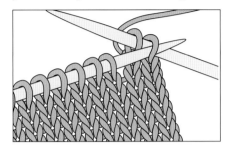

1 Knit the first two stitches in the usual way. Slip the tip of the left-hand needle into the first stitch you knitted onto the right-hand needle. Lift it over the second stitch you knitted and drop it off the needle. You now have only one stitch on the right-hand needle.

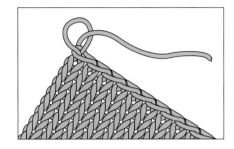

3 Cut the yarn, leaving a 10cm (4in) tail to sew in later. Put the cut end through the remaining stitch and pull it tight.

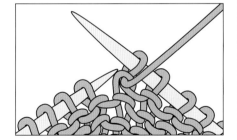

4 Slip the original stitch off the left-hand needle. The purled stitch is now complete.

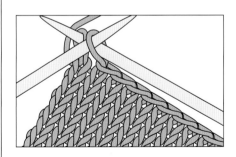

2 Knit another stitch onto the right-hand needle and then pass the previous stitch you knitted over it. Continue in this way until you have one stitch remaining on the right-hand needle.

Increasing One Stitch (inc)

How to make an extra stitch on the needles.

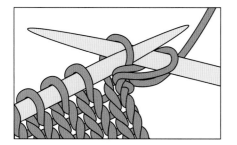

1 Work to the position of the increase. Knit into the front of the next stitch in the usual way, but do not slip the original stitch off the left-hand needle. Put the tip of the right-hand needle into the back of the same stitch on the left-hand needle.

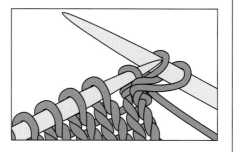

3 Bring the needle, and the loop of yarn wrapped around it, through the stitch, and now slip the original stitch off the left-hand needle. You have made two stitches out of one and so increased by one stitch.

Knit Two Stitches Together (k2tog)

How to make one fewer stitches on the needle.

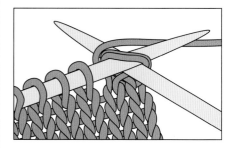

1 From front to back, put the tip of the right-hand needle into the next two stitches on the left-hand needle. Knit the two stitches together in the usual way as if they were one. You have made two stitches into one and so decreased by one stitch.

To knit three stitches together, simply put the right-hand needle through three instead of two stitches.

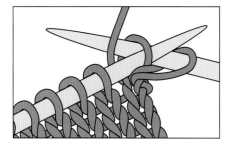

2 Wrap the yarn around the right-hand needle in the same way you would to knit a stitch.

Abbreviations

alt alternate
approx approximately
beg begin(ning)
cm centimetre(s)
cont continue
foll(s) follow(s)(ing)
g gram(s)
icos including cast (bound) off stitch. After casting (binding) off the stated number of stitches, one stitch remains on the right-hand needle. This stitch is included in the number of the following group of stitches.
in inches
inc work into front and back of next stitch to increase by one stitch
k knit
k2(3)tog knit next two (three) stitches together
oz ounces
p purl
p2(3)tog purl next two (three) stitches together
rem remain(ing)
rep repeat
RS right side
sk2po slip one stitch, knit two stitches together, pass slipped stitch over
st(s) stitch(es)
st st stocking (stockinette) stitch
w&t wrap and turn. See Wrap and Turn Method, right.
WS wrong side
[ ] work instructions within square brackets as directed
***** work instructions after asterisk(s) as directed

Colour Knitting

There are two main techniques for working with more than one colour in the same row of knitting: the intarsia technique and the Fair Isle technique.

Intarsia Technique

This method is used when knitting individual, large blocks of colour, as in the Simple Dog and the face of the Simple Cat. It is best to use a small ball (or long length) for each area of colour, otherwise the yarn will easily become tangled. When changing to a new colour, twist the yarns on the wrong side of the work to prevent holes forming.

When starting a new row, turn the knitting so that the yarns that are hanging from it untwist as much as possible. If you have several colours you may occasionally have to reorganize the yarns at the back of the knitting. Your work may look messy but once the ends are all sewn in it will look fine.

Fair Isle (or Stranding) Technique

If there are no more than four stitches between colours you can use the Fair Isle technique, for instance on the head of the Ferret.

Begin knitting with the first colour, then drop this when you introduce the second colour. When you come to the first colour again, take it under the second colour to twist the yarns. When you come to the second colour again, take it over the first colour. The secret is not to pull the strands on the wrong side of the work too tightly or the work will pucker.

Wrap and Turn Method (w&t)

Use this method for the head of the Ferret, Hamster and Shetland Pony. Once you have mastered this technique you will be able to knit all the dogs, cats and wild animals from our other books. Knit the number of stitches in the first short row. Slip the next stitch purlwise from the left-hand to the right-hand needle. Bring the yarn forward then slip the stitch back onto the left-hand needle. Return the yarn to the back. On a purl row use the same method, taking the yarn back then forward.

Short Row Patterning

Use this method for working the head of the Shetland Pony.

Short Row Patterning is worked as Wrap and Turn, but the number of stitches worked is decreased by one stitch a row for as many rows as in the pattern, then increased to the original number of stitches.

Scarf Fringe Method

Use this method for the mane of the Shetland Pony.

Cut yarn as required and fold each piece in half. Slip a crochet hook through a stitch, hook the folded end of yarn through the stitch, slip the ends through the loop and pull the yarn tightly. Once all fringing has been done, cut to correct length.

Wrapping Pipecleaners In Yarn

This method is used for the legs and beak of the Canary and Parrot: if possible use coloured pipe cleaners and try to match the colour of the wrapping yarn. Leaving a 5cm (2in) tail of free yarn, tightly wrap the yarn around the pipecleaner, making sure no pipecleaner chenille pokes through. Continue wrapping down the pipecleaner to as close to the tip as possible, then wrap the yarn back up to the top of the pipecleaner. Knot the two ends and slip them in to the body. If there is a little bit of white pipecleaner chenille showing, colour in with a matching felt-tip pen. A little dab of clear glue will stop the wrapping slipping off the end of the pipecleaner.

Whiskers

We recommend using 5cm (2in) lengths of transparent nylon thread. To stop them falling out, dab a small amount of clear glue on both sides of the cheeks.

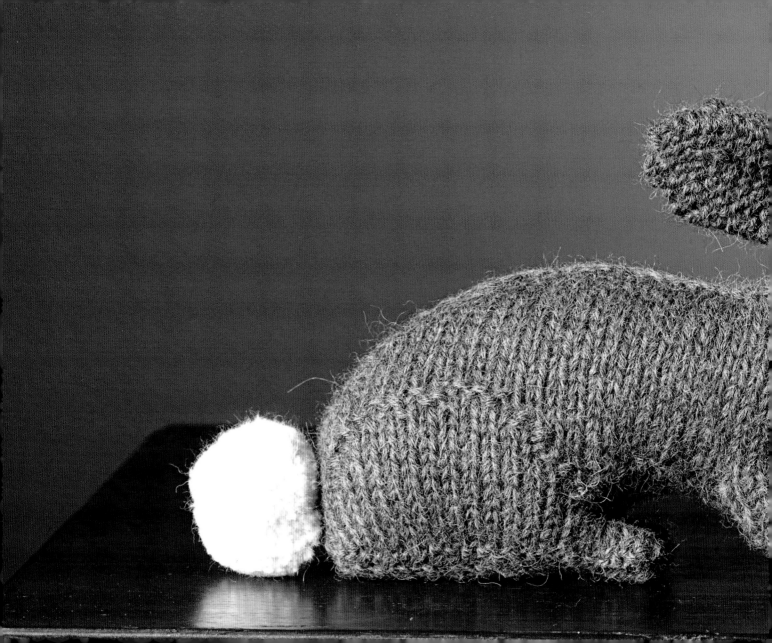

Small
And
Furry

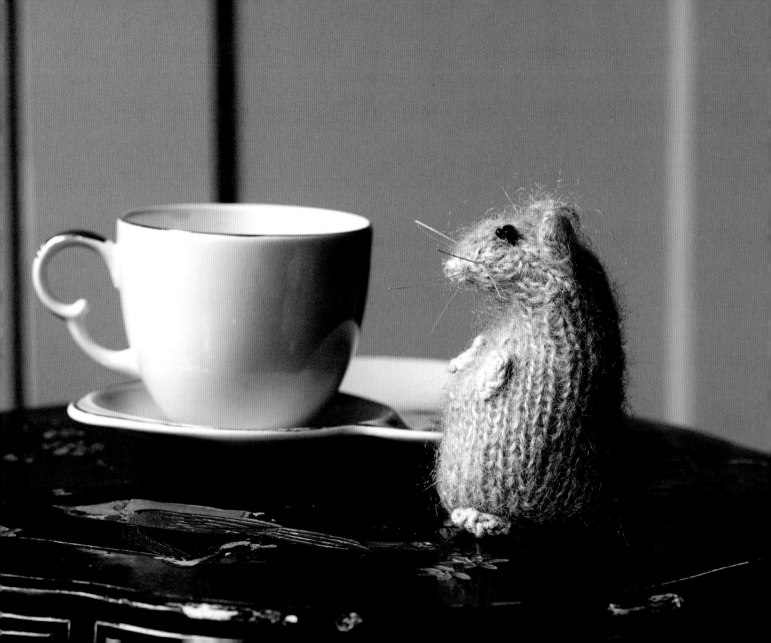

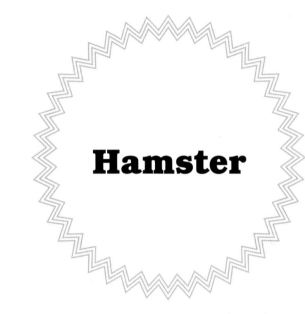

Hamster

The word hamster comes from the German *hamstern* meaning 'to hoard'. Hamsters can hoard an enormous amount of food in their cheek pouches and have even been known to hide their pups in their pouches if they sense danger. They make lovely pets, although ours were a bit unrewarding – they slept all day and spent all night noisily pounding around on their wheel. Apparently Sid Vicious was named after Johnny Rotten's hamster.

Hamster 🏅🏅

If you fill the hamster with lentils he will sit in your hand like the real thing.

Measurements

Height: 10cm (4in)
Width: 6cm (2½in)

Materials

Pair of 3¼mm (US 3) knitting needles
Pair of 2¼mm (US 1) knitting needles
15g (½oz) of Rowan Kidsilk Haze Trio in Snowberry 790 (sn)
5g (⅛oz) of Rowan Wool Cotton in Tender 951 (te) for nose and paws
Tiny amount of Rowan Pure Wool 4ply in Black 404 (bl) for eyes
Fishing line for whiskers
Lentils for stuffing

Abbreviations

See page 12.
See page 13 for Wrap and Turn Method.

The hamster is just the right size to put in your pocket.

Body

With 3¼mm (US 3) needles and sn, cast on 1 st.
Row 1: Inc knitwise. *(2 sts)*
Row 2: Knit.
Row 3: [Inc knitwise] twice. *(4 sts)*
Beg with a k row, work 2 rows st st.
Row 6: K4, cast on 10 sts. *(14 sts)*
Row 7: P14, cast on 10 sts. *(24 sts)*
Work 6 rows st st.
Row 14: K5, inc, k12, inc, k5. *(26 sts)*
Row 15: Purl.
Row 16: K5, inc, k14, inc, k5. *(28 sts)*
Work 5 rows st st.
Row 22: K2tog, k7, k2tog, k6, k2tog, k7, k2tog. *(24 sts)*
Work 5 rows st st.
Row 28: K2tog, k6, k2tog, k4, k2tog, k6, k2tog. *(20 sts)*
Work 3 rows st st.
Row 32: K2tog, k16, k2tog. *(18 sts)*
Work 3 rows st st.
Row 36: K14 wrap and turn (leave 4 sts on left-hand needle unworked).
Row 37: Working top of head on centre 10 sts only, p10, w&t.

Row 38: K10, w&t.
Row 39: P10, w&t.
Row 40: K10, w&t.
Row 41: P10, w&t.
Row 42: K across all sts. *(18 sts in total)*
Row 43: P2tog, p14, p2tog. *(16 sts)*
Row 44: K12, w&t (leave 4 sts on left-hand needle unworked).
Row 45: P8, w&t.
Row 46: K8, w&t.
Row 47: P8, w&t.
Row 48: K across all sts. *(16 sts in total)*
Row 49: P2tog, p2, p2tog, p4, p2tog, p2, p2tog. *(12 sts)*
Row 50: K2, k2tog, k4, k2tog, k2. *(10 sts)*
Row 51: [P2tog] 5 times. *(5 sts)*
Row 52: K2tog, k1, k2tog. *(3 sts)*
Row 53: P3tog and fasten off.

Ear

(make 2 the same)
With 3¼mm (US 3) needles and sn, cast on 5 sts.
Beg with a k row, work 4 rows st st.
Row 5: K2tog, k1, k2tog. *(3 sts)*
Row 6: P3tog and fasten off.

Back Paws

(make 2 the same)
With 2¼mm (US 1) needles and te, cast on 5 sts.
Work 4 rows st st.
Row 5: K2tog, k1, k2tog. *(3 sts)*
Work 2 rows st st.
Row 8: P3tog and fasten off.

Front Paws

(make 2 the same)
With 2¼mm (US 1) needles and te, cast on 3 sts.
Beg with a k row, work 3 rows st st.
Cast (bind) off.

To Make Up

SEWING IN ENDS Sew in ends, leaving ends from cast on and cast (bound) off rows for sewing up.

BODY With RS together, starting after tail (from row 6), sew up body, leaving a 2.5cm (1in) gap.

STUFFING Stuff head and top of body firmly, adding lentils to bottom of body for weight. Sew up gap.

NOSE With te, embroider 3 parallel satin stitches, positioned as in photograph.

EYES With bl, sew 3-loop French knots, positioned as in photograph.

PAWS Sew back paws to underside of body, with RS facing up, approx 1 st each side of centre seam. Sew front paws, as photograph, approx 1st either side of centre seam.

EARS Attach ears to top of head, with RS facing forwards and with 4 sts between.

WHISKERS Cut 3 x 8cm (3in) lengths of fishing line and thread through cheeks. Trim.

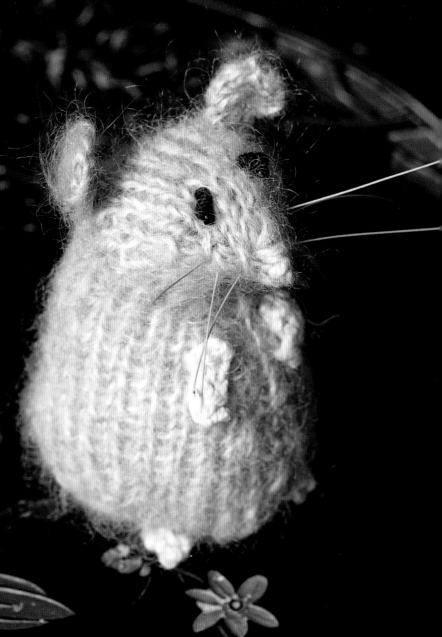

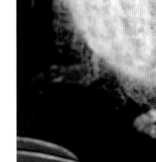

PAWS

The hamster has tiny front paws sewn to the front of his body.

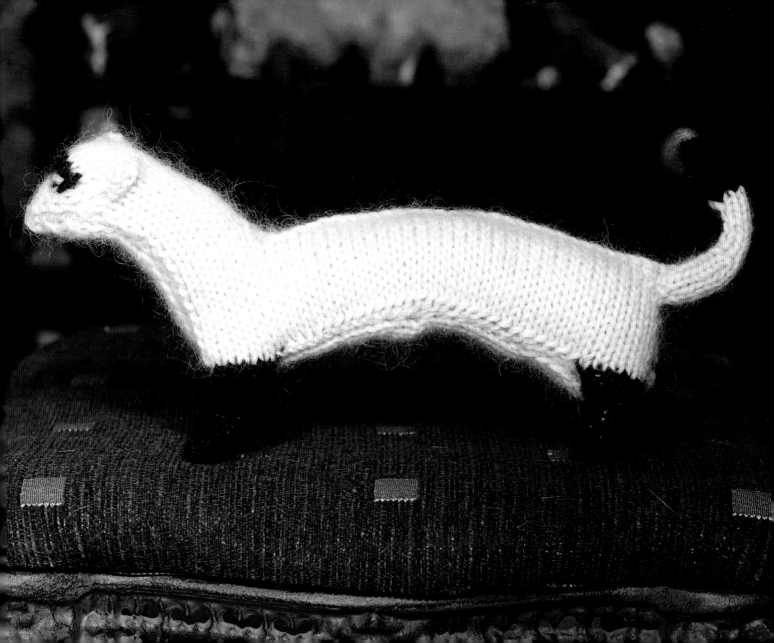

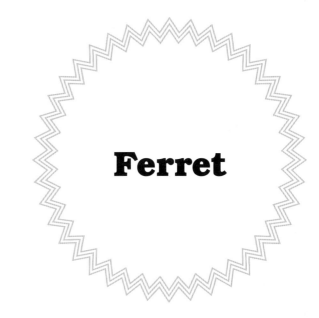

Ferret

'Ferret-legging' is the ancient sport of keeping a ferret down one's trousers. The world record is five hours and thirty minutes. Draco Malfoy was turned into an albino ferret in the fourth Harry Potter book. Ferrets are alleged to make loving and friendly pets, but as they have four different sets of teeth it's perhaps a good idea to stick to the knitted version.

Ferret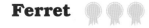

The ferret is knitted with doubled yarn, which makes him quick to make.

Measurements
Length including tail: 33cm (13in)
Height to top of head: 12cm (4¾in)

Materials
Pair of 3¼mm (US 3) knitting needles
Double-pointed 3¼mm (US 3) knitting needles (for holding stitches)
15g (½oz) of Rowan Kid Classic in Peat 832 (pe) used DOUBLE throughout
40g (1½oz) of Rowan Kid Classic in Feather 828 (fe) used DOUBLE throughout
2 pipecleaners for legs and tail
Fishing line for whiskers

Abbreviations
See page 12.
See page 13 for Intarsia Technique.
See page 13 for Wrap and Turn Method.

HEAD
The ferret has a stripe across his eyes like a bandit.

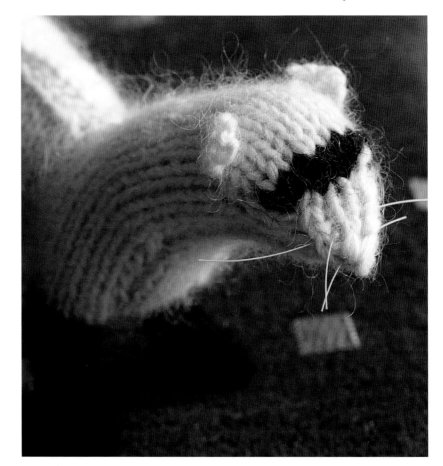

Right Back Leg

With pe, cast on 10 sts.

Beg with a k row, work 2 rows st st.

Row 3: K2, k2tog, k2, k2tog, k2. *(8 sts)*

Row 4: Purl.

Work 4 rows st st.

Row 9: K2, inc, k2, inc, k2. *(10 sts)*

Row 10: Purl.

Row 11: K2, inc, k4, inc, k2. *(12 sts)*

Row 12: Purl.*

Row 13: Cast (bind) off 6 sts, k to end (hold 6 sts on spare needle for Right Side of Body).

Left Back Leg

Work as for Right Back Leg to *.

Row 13: K6, cast (bind) off 6 sts (hold 6 sts on spare needle for Left Side of Body).

Right Front Leg

With pe, cast on 10 sts.

Beg with a k row, work 2 rows st st.

Row 3: K2, k2tog, k2, k2tog, k2. *(8 sts)*

Row 4: Purl.

Work 8 rows st st.

Row 13: K2, inc, k2, inc, k2. *(10 sts)*

Row 14: Purl.

Row 15: K2, inc, k4, inc, k2. *(12 sts)*

Row 16: Purl.*

Row 17: Cast (bind) off 6 sts, k to end (hold 6 sts on spare needle for Right Side of Body).

Left Front Leg

Work as for Right Front Leg to *.

Row 17: K6, cast (bind) off 6 sts (hold 6 sts on spare needle for Left Side of Body).

Right Side of Body

With fe, cast on 1 st, with RS facing k6 from spare needle of Right Front Leg, cast on 28 sts, k6 from spare needle of Right Back Leg. *(41 sts)*

Row 2: Purl.

Work 10 rows st st.

Row 13: K8 (hold 8 sts on spare needle for right neck), cast (bind) off 14 sts, k17 icos, k2tog. *(18 sts)*

Row 14: P2tog, p14, p2tog. *(16 sts)*

Cast (bind) off 16 sts.

Left Side of Body

With fe, cast on 1 st, with WS facing p6 from spare needle of Left Front Leg, cast on 28 sts, p6 from spare needle of Left Back Leg. *(41 sts)*

Row 2: Knit.

Work 10 rows st st.

Row 13: P8 (hold 8 sts on spare needle for left neck), cast (bind) off 14 sts, p17 icos, p2tog. *(18 sts)*

Row 14: K2tog, k14, k2tog. *(16 sts)*

Cast (bind) off 16 sts.

Neck and Head

With RS facing and fe, k8 held for neck from spare needle of Right Side of Body, then k8 held for neck from spare needle of Left Side of Body. *(16 sts)*

Row 2: P7, p2tog, p7. *(15 sts)*

Work 6 rows st st.

Row 9: K5, k2tog, k1, k2tog, k5. *(13 sts)*

Work 5 rows st st.

Row 15: K10, wrap and turn (leave 3 sts on left-hand needle unworked).

Row 16: Working on centre 7 sts only, p7, w&t.

Row 17: K7, w&t.

Rep rows 16–17 once more.

Row 20: P7, w&t.

Row 21: Knit across all sts. *(13 sts in total)*

Join in pe.

Row 22: P2togfe, p1fe, p7pe, p1fe, p2togfe. *(11 sts)*

Row 23: K3fe, 5pe, 3fe.

Cont in fe only.

Row 24: P2, p2tog, p3, p2tog, p2. *(9 sts)*

Row 25: K2, k2tog, k1, k2tog, k2. *(7 sts)*

Row 26: P1, p2tog, p1, p2tog, p1. *(5 sts)*

Why not change the colour of the yarn and make a stoat or a weasel instead?

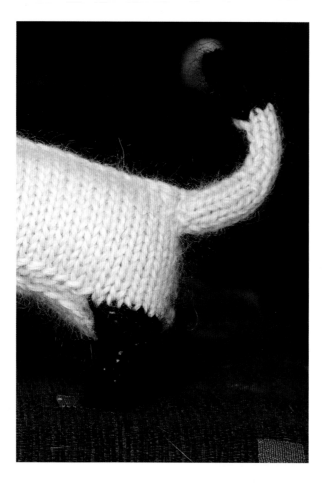

Row 27: Knit.
Row 28: P2tog, p1, p2tog. *(3 sts)*
Row 29: K3tog and fasten off.

Tummy

With fe, cast on 4 sts.
Beg with a k row, work 4 rows st st.
Row 5: K1, [inc] twice, k1. *(6 sts)*
Work 77 rows st st.
Row 83: K2tog, k2, k2tog. *(4 sts)*
Row 84: Purl.
Row 85: [K2tog] twice. *(2 sts)*
Row 86: P2.
Row 87: K2tog and fasten off.

Ear

(make 2 the same)
With fe, cast on 5 sts.
Row 1: Knit
Row 2: P2tog, p1, p2tog. *(3 sts)*
Cast (bind) off.

Tail

With pe, cast on 5 sts.
Beg with a k row, work 6 rows st st.
Join in fe.
Work 10 rows st st.
Row 17: K1, inc, k1, inc, k1. *(7 sts)*
Row 18: Purl.
Work 6 rows st st.
Cast (bind) off.

MARKINGS
The ferret has dark brown legs
and tip to his tail.

To Make Up

SEWING IN ENDS Sew in ends leaving ends from cast on and cast (bound) off rows for sewing up.

LEGS With WS together sew up seam on outside. Cut a pipecleaner to approximately the length of both front legs, leaving an extra 2.5cm (1in) at both ends, fold over 2.5cm (1in) each end. With a little stuffing wrapped around, push the folded end of pipecleaner into each leg,

BODY Sew along back of ferret and down its bottom.

TAIL Cut a pipecleaner 2.5cm (1in) longer than tail. Roll a little stuffing around pipecleaner, wrap tail around pipecleaner and sew up tail on RS, attach tail to top of bottom, with approx 3cm (1¼in) of pipecleaner sticking into the body.

TUMMY Sew cast on row of tummy to bottom of ferret's bottom and cast (bound) off row to ferret's nose. Ease and sew tummy to fit – the tummy is slightly shorter than the body so will pull the head down. Leave a 2.5cm (1in) gap between front and back legs on one side.

STUFFING Stuff the ferret firmly starting with head, and sew up the gap. Mould the body into shape.

EARS Sew cast on row of each ear to side of ferret's head, 6 rows back from mask, with 4 sts between the ears.

WHISKERS Cut 3 x 8cm (3in) lengths of fishing line and thread through cheeks. Trim.

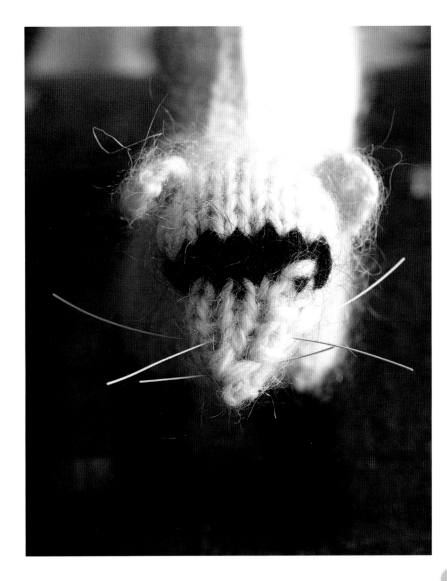

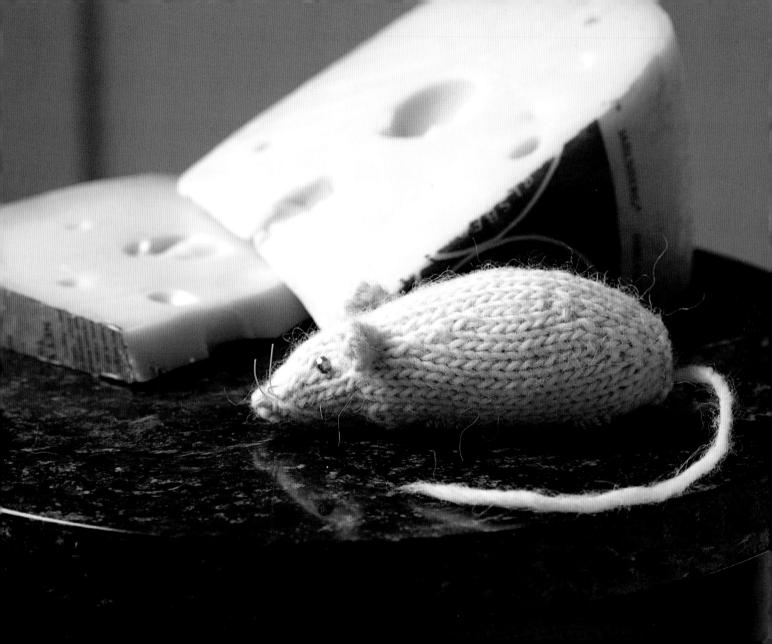

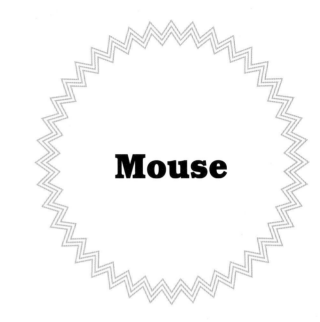

Mouse

Mice are either adorable or terrifying. Ours is knitted and therefore adorable. The word 'mouse' means thief; anyone who has had a mouse infestation will understand why. Fried mice or mouse pie used to be used as a cure for bedwetting. Female mice can produce more than 120 babies a year, and their tails are the same length as their bodies. The best known mouse is Mickey, closely followed by Jerry.

Mouse

The mouse is very quick and easy to knit.

Measurements
Length: 11cm (4¼in)
Height: 4cm (1¼in)

Materials
Pair of 3¼mm (US 3) knitting needles
10g (¼oz) of Rowan Creative Focus Worsted in Natural 100 (na)
Tiny amount of Rowan Wool Cotton in Tender 951 (te) for nose and paws
2 tiny pink beads for eyes and sewing needle and pink thread for sewing on
Fishing line for whiskers

Abbreviations
See page 12.

Body
With na, cast on 16 sts.
Beg with a k row, work 2 rows st st.
Row 3: K5, inc, k4, inc, k5. *(18 sts)*
Row 4: Purl.
Row 5: K6, inc, k4, inc, k6. *(20 sts)*
Row 6: Purl.
Row 7: K7, inc, k4, inc, k7. *(22 sts)*
Row 8: Purl.
Row 9: K9, inc, k2, inc, k9. *(24 sts)*
Row 10: Purl.
Row 11: K10, inc, k2, inc, k10. *(26 sts)*
Row 12: Purl.
Work 4 rows st st.
Row 17: K9, k2tog, k4, k2tog, k9. *(24 sts)*
Row 18: Purl.
Row 19: K8, k2tog, k4, k2tog, k8. *(22 sts)*
Row 20: Purl.
Row 21: K7, k2tog, k4, k2tog, k7. *(20 sts)*
Row 22: Purl.

Work 2 rows st st.
Row 25: [K2tog, k2] 5 times. *(15 sts)*
Row 26: P2tog, p2, p2tog, p3, p2tog, p2, p2tog. *(11 sts)*
Row 27: K4, inc, k1, inc, k4. *(13 sts)*
Work 3 rows st st.
Row 31: [K1, k2tog] 4 times, k1. *(9 sts)*
Row 32: Purl.
Row 33: [K2tog, k1] 3 times. *(6 sts)*
Row 34: [P2tog] 3 times. *(3 sts)*
Row 35: K3tog and fasten off.

Ear
(make 2 the same)
With na, cast on 5 sts.
Row 1: K1, k2tog, k2. *(4 sts)*
Row 2: Purl.
Row 3: K1, k2tog k1. *(3 sts)*
Row 4: P3tog and fasten off.

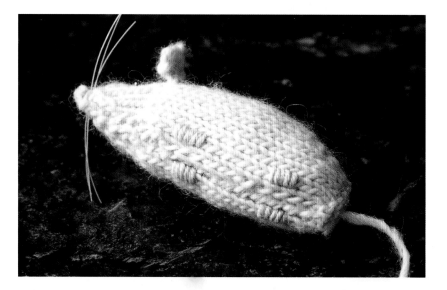

FEET
The mouse's feet are embroidered on with pink yarn.

To Make Up

SEWING IN ENDS Sew in ends, leaving ends from cast on and cast (bound) off rows for sewing up.

BODY, STUFFING AND TAIL With RS facing and starting at nose, sew up body leaving a 2.5cm (1in gap) gap, stuff, sew up gap, and at bottom leave approx 14cm (5½in) of sewing-up yarn for tail.

EARS Sew cast (bound) off row of ears to top of mouse, with WS facing forward, with 3 sts between ears and approx 8 rows back from nose.

PAWS With te, make 5 parallel rows of 5mm (¼in) satin stitches 1 st either side of centre seam, 6 and 17 rows from bottom seam.

NOSE With te, embroider 5 parallel satin sts, as in photograph.

EYES Sew on 2 pink beads for eyes, approximately 3 rows in front of ears, with 4 sts between them.

WHISKERS Cut 3 x 8cm (3in) lengths of fishing line and thread through cheeks. Trim.

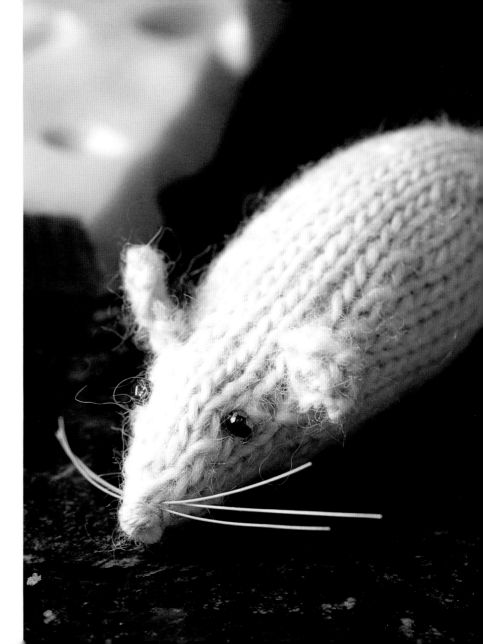

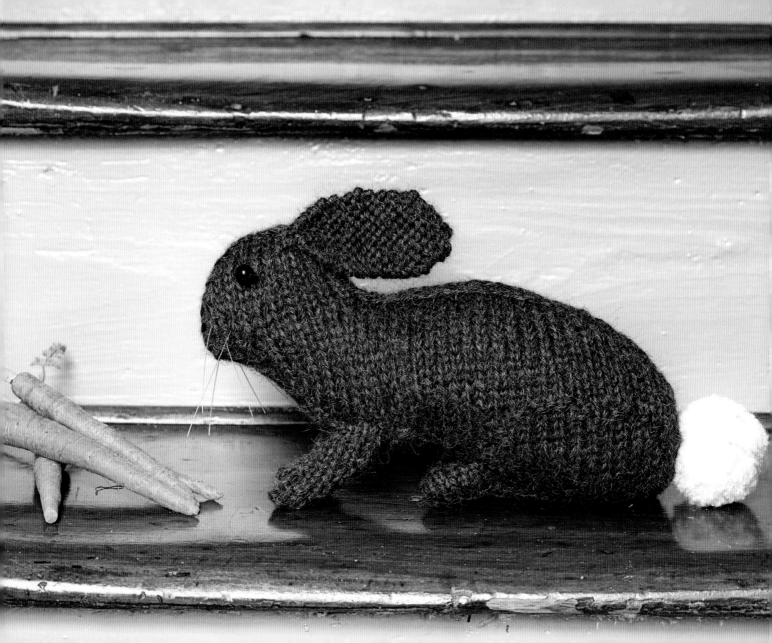

Rabbit

One of the most recognisable and loved of all pets, rabbits are cute, soft, friendly and cuddly.

In the wild they live in a warren of burrows; as pets they are kept in hutches, but are equally happy indoors. Rabbits are popular characters in literature and cartoons: Peter Rabbit, Bugs Bunny, The White Rabbit from *Alice In Wonderland*, *Watership Down*, Bunnykins. The Easter Bunny, rather like Father Christmas, brings chocolate eggs to children at Easter. Bunny Girls serve drinks at the Playboy Club, dressed in a leotard, with bow tie and ears, and even a cottontail.

Rabbit

Fairly simple to make and knitted in lovely soft alpaca yarn.

Measurements
Length: 26cm (10¼in)
Height to top of ears: 21cm (8¼in)

Materials
Pair of 4mm (US 6) knitting needles
Pair of 3¼mm (US 3) knitting needles (for ears)
Double-pointed 4mm (US 6) knitting needles (for holding stitches)
40g (1½oz) of Rowan Baby Alpaca DK in Lincoln 209 (li) used DOUBLE throughout
10g (¼oz) of Rowan Baby Alpaca DK in Jacob 205 (ja) for pompom tail
Tiny amount of Rowan Pure Wool 4ply in Black 404 (bl) for nose
2 black wooden beads for eyes and sewing needle and black thread for sewing on
Fishing line for whiskers
1 pipecleaner for front legs

Abbreviations
See page 12.

Right Front Leg
With 4mm (US 6) needles and li, cast on 6 sts.
Work 2 rows st st.
Row 3: Inc, [k2tog] twice, inc. *(6 sts)*
Work 5 rows st st.
Row 9: Inc, k4, inc. *(8 sts)*
Work 3 rows st st.*

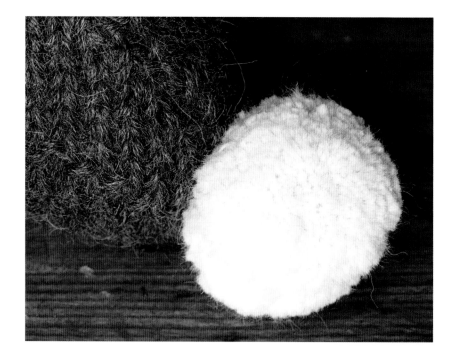

Row 13: Cast (bind) off 4 sts, k to end (hold 4 sts on spare needle for Right Side of Body).

Left Front Leg
Work as for Right Front Leg to *.
Row 13: K4, cast (bind) off 4 sts (hold 4 sts on spare needle for Left Side of Body).

Right Side of Body
With 4mm (US 6) needles and li, cast on 22 sts.
Beg with a k row, work 4 rows st st.
Shape back leg
Row 5: K5, turn.
Work on these 5 sts only for Right Back Leg.

TAIL
When knotting the centre of the pom-pom, keep the yarn ends long and use them to attach the pom-pom to the rabbit's bottom.

Beg with a p row, work 2 rows st st.
Cast (bind) off.
Row 5: Rejoin yarn to rem 17 sts, k to end.
Row 6: P3, k1, p13.
Row 7: Inc, p1, k11, p1, k3. *(18 sts)*
Row 8: P2tog, p2, k1, p10, k1, p1, inc. *(18 sts)*
Row 9: Inc, k2, p1, k10, p1, k3. *(19 sts)*
Row 10: P4, k1, p8, k1, p4, inc. *(20 sts)*
Row 11: Inc, k5, p1, k6, p2, k5. *(21 sts)*
Row 12: P2tog, p6, k1, p3, k1, p7, inc. *(21 sts)*
Row 13: Inc, k9, p3, k8. *(22 sts)*
Row 14: P2tog, p19, inc, p4 from spare needle of Right Front Leg, cast on 1 st. *(27 sts)*
Row 15: Inc, k26. *(28 sts)*
Row 16: P2tog, p26. *(27 sts)*
Row 17: Inc, k26. *(28 sts)*
Row 18: P2tog, p26. *(27 sts)*
Row 19: Inc, k26. *(28 sts)*
Row 20: P2tog, p26. *(27 sts)*
Row 21: Knit.
Row 22: P2tog, p25. *(26 sts)*
Row 23: K24, k2tog. *(25 sts)*
Row 24: P2tog, p23. *(24 sts)*
Row 25: K22, k2tog. *(23 sts)*
Shape head
Row 26: Cast (bind) off 15 sts, p to end, cast on 5 sts. *(13 sts)*
Work 3 rows st st.
Row 30: P11, p2tog. *(12 sts)*
Work 2 rows st st.
Row 33: K2tog, k8, k2tog. *(10 sts)*
Row 34: Purl.
Row 35: K2tog, k8. *(9 sts)*
Row 36: P7, p2tog. *(8 sts)*
Cast (bind) off.

Left Side of Body
With 4mm (US 6) needles and li, cast on 22 sts.
Beg with a p row, work 4 rows st st.
Shape back leg
Row 5: P5, turn.
Work on these 5 sts only for Left Back Leg.
Beg with a k row, work 2 rows st st.

Cast (bind) off.
Row 5: Working on rem 17 sts, rejoin yarn, purl to end.
Row 6: K3, p1, k13.
Row 7: Inc, k1, p11, k1, p3. *(18 sts)*
Row 8: K2tog, k2, p1, k10, p1, k1, inc. *(18 sts)*
Row 9: Inc, p2, k1, p10, k1, p3. *(19 sts)*
Row 10: K4, p1, k8, p1, k4, inc. *(20 sts)*
Row 11: Inc, p5, k1, p6, k2, p5. *(21 sts)*
Row 12: K2tog, k6, p1, k3, p1, k7, inc. *(21 sts)*
Row 13: Inc, p9, k3, p8. *(22 sts)*
Row 14: K2tog, k19, inc, pick up and k4 from spare needle of Left Front Leg, cast on 1 st. *(27 sts)*
Row 15: Inc, p26. *(28 sts)*
Row 16: K2tog, k26. *(27 sts)*
Row 17: Inc, p26. *(28 sts)*
Row 18: K2tog, k26. *(27 sts)*
Row 19: Inc, p26. *(28 sts)*
Row 20: K2tog, k26. *(27 sts)*
Row 21: Purl.
Row 22: K2tog, k25. *(26 sts)*
Row 23: P24, p2tog. *(25 sts)*
Row 24: K2tog, k23. *(24 sts)*
Row 25: P22, p2tog. *(23 sts)*
Shape head
Row 26: Cast (bind) off 15 sts, k to end, cast on 5 sts. *(13 sts)*
Work 3 rows st st.
Row 30: K11, k2tog. *(12 sts)*
Work 2 rows st st.
Row 33: P2tog, p8, p2tog. *(10 sts)*
Row 34: Knit.

Our rabbit is grey, but you could make yours any colour you wanted.

EARS

You can arrange the rabbit's ears to be floppy if you prefer.

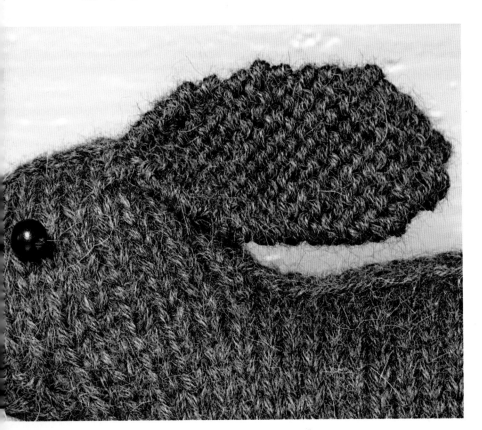

Row 35: P2tog, p8. *(9 sts)*
Row 36: K7, k2tog. *(8 sts)*
Cast (bind) off.

Tummy

With 4mm (US 6) needles and li, cast on
4 sts.
Beg with a k row, work 56 rows st st.
Cast (bind) off.

Ear

(make 2 the same)
With 3¼mm (US 3) needles and li, cast on
6 sts.
Knit 4 rows.
Row 5: K1, inc, k2, inc, k1. *(8 sts)*
Knit 18 rows.
Row 24: K2tog, k4, k2tog. *(6 sts)*
Knit 2 rows.
Row 27: K2tog, k2, k2tog. *(4 sts)*
Row 28: Knit.
Cast (bind) off.

Tail

With ja, make a pom-pom.
Cut two 4cm (1¼in) cardboard discs and cut
a 2cm (¾in) hole in the centre of each. Hold
the discs together and wind the yarn
around the ring as evenly as possible until
the hole is almost filled with yarn (it is
quicker to wind several strands at once).
Then thread yarn onto a needle and
continue to wind until the hole is closed up.
Cut the yarn around the edge of the circles.
Ease the cardboard discs slightly apart and
wrap a long length of doubled yarn between
them and around the centre of the pom-
pom. Tie the pom-pom together tightly at the
centre, leaving a long tail of yarn to use for
attaching pom-pom to rabbit. Then cut the
cardboard away from the pom-pom. Fluff up
the pom-pom and, if necessary, trim.

To Make Up

SEWING IN ENDS Sew in ends, leaving ends from cast on and cast (bound) off rows for sewing up.

LEGS With WS together, fold leg in half and sew up leg on RS.

BODY Sew around bottom, along body, around head to halfway down front chest of rabbit.

TUMMY Sew cast on row of tummy to bottom of rabbit's bottom, and sew cast (bound) off row to halfway up front chest. Ease and sew tummy to fit body. Leave a 2.5cm (1in) gap between front and back legs on one side.

STUFFING Pipecleaners are used to stiffen the front legs. Fold a pipecleaner into a U-shape and measure against two front legs. Cut to fit approximately, leaving an extra 2.5cm (1in) at both ends. Fold these ends over to stop pipecleaner poking out of paws. Roll a little stuffing around pipecleaner and slip into body and down front legs. Starting at the head, stuff the rabbit, then sew up the gap. Mould body into shape.

EARS Slightly pinch the bottom of the ear and sew cast on row to rabbit's head, leaving 1cm (½in) between each ear. For standing up ears, sew together at the tip: alternatively, let the ears flop for a flop-eared rabbit.

TAIL Attach pom-pom to base of bottom.

EYES With black thread, sew two black beads onto head as shown in photograph, or use black yarn.

NOSE With bl, embroider two vertical stitches, followed by two horizontal stitches on one side and two stitches on the other side.

WHISKERS Cut 3 x 8cm (3in) lengths of fishing line and thread through cheeks. Trim.

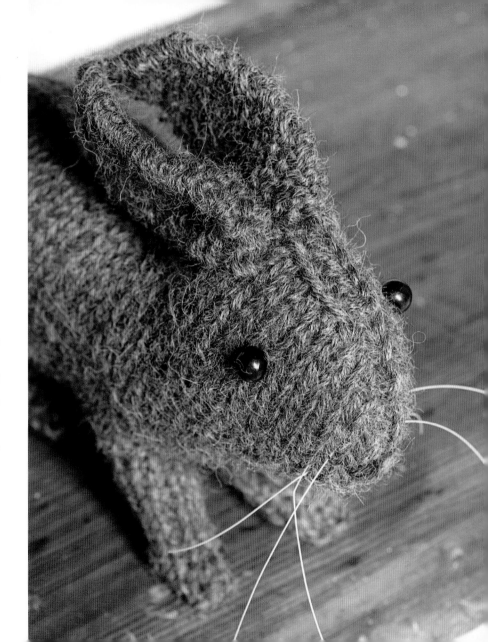

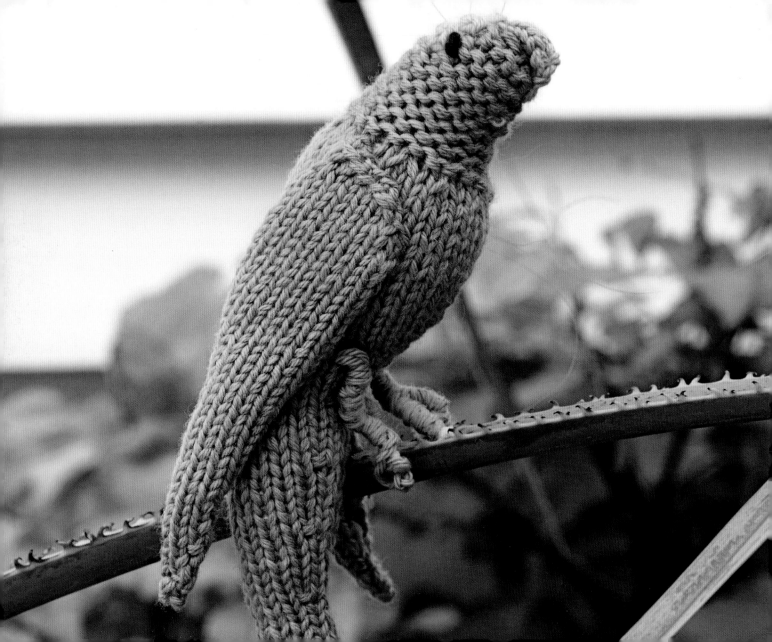

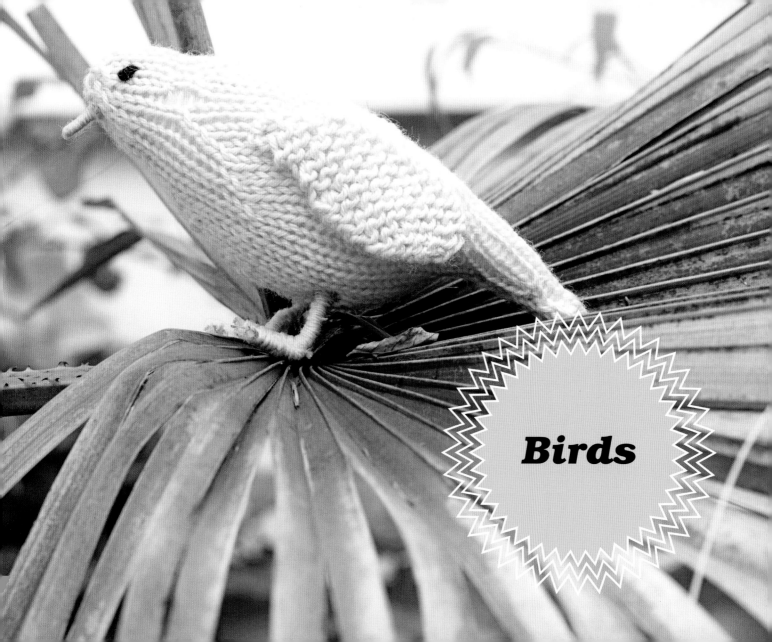

Birds

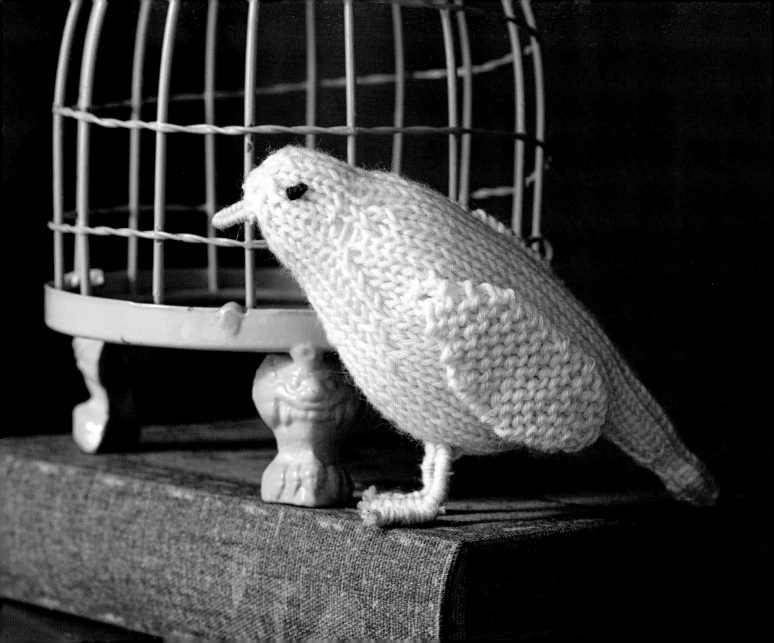

Canary

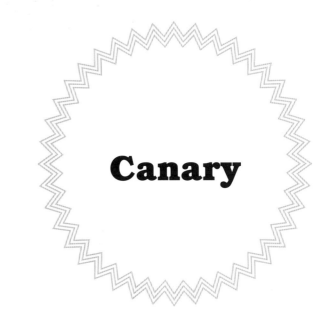

The canary is a small songbird with a lovely singing voice, so lovely they became popular pets in European courts. They were also useful as an early warning system in the coal mines; toxic gases would affect the canary first and he would sadly die. The main character in the cartoon *Tweety Bird* is a canary. Norwich City football team's nickname is The Canaries, because Norwich was famous for breeding and exporting the birds.

Canary

Knitted all in one piece, apart from the wings, the canary is a quick knit.

Measurements
Length: 17cm (7in)
Height to top of head: 10cm (4in)

Materials
Pair of 3¼mm (US 3) knitting needles
15g (½oz) of Rowan Baby Merino Silk DK in Limone 675 (le)
2 pipecleaners for legs and tail
Tiny amount of Rowan Pure Wool 4ply in Black 404 (bl) for eyes
Small amount of Rowan Pure Wool 4ply in Shell 468 (sh) for beak and legs

Abbreviations
See page 12.

Tail and Body
(starting at the tail)
With le, cast on 6 sts.
Beg with a k row, work 8 rows st st.
Row 9: K1, inc, k2, inc, k1. *(8 sts)*
Work 7 rows st st.
Row 17: K1, inc, k4, inc, k1. *(10 sts)*
Row 18 and every foll alt row to row 54: Purl.
Row 19: Inc, k1, inc, k4, inc, k1, inc. *(14 sts)*
Row 21: Inc, k2, inc, k6, inc, k2, inc. *(18 sts)*
Row 23: Inc, k2, inc, k10, inc, k2, inc. *(22 sts)*
Row 25: Inc, k3, inc, k12, inc, k3, inc. *(26 sts)*

Row 27: Inc, k5, inc, k12, inc, k5, inc. *(30 sts)*
Work 5 rows st st.
Row 33: K10, inc, k8, inc, k10. *(32 sts)*
Row 35: K10, inc, k10, inc, k10. *(34 sts)*
Row 37: K10, inc, k12, inc, k10. *(36 sts)*
Row 39: K2tog, k4, k2tog, k20, k2tog, k4, k2tog. *(32 sts)*
Row 41: K2tog, k4, k2tog, k16, k2tog, k4, k2tog. *(28 sts)*
Row 43: K2tog, k4, k2tog, k12, k2tog, k4, k2tog. *(24 sts)*
Row 45: K2tog, k3, k2tog, k2, k2tog, k2, k2tog, k2, k2tog, k3, k2tog. *(18 sts)*
Row 47: K4, k2tog twice, k2, k2tog twice, k4. *(14 sts)*
Row 49: K5, inc, k2, inc, k5. *(16 sts)*
Work 5 rows st st.
Row 55: K2tog, k1, k2tog, k2, k2tog, k2, k2tog, k1, k2tog. *(11 sts)*
Row 56: P2tog, p1, p2tog, p1, p2tog, p1, p2tog. *(7 sts)*
Row 57: K2tog twice, k1, k2tog. *(4 sts)*
Break yarn leaving long end, thread end through open sts, pull tight and secure.

Wing
(make 2 the same)
With le, cast on 4 sts.
Knit 2 rows.
Row 3: Inc, k3. *(5 sts)*
Knit 1 row.

Row 5: Inc, k4. *(6 sts)*
Knit 1 row.
Row 7: Inc, k5. *(7 sts)*
Knit 10 rows.
Row 18: K5, k2tog. *(6 sts)*
Knit 3 rows.
Row 22: K2tog, k2, k2tog. *(4 sts)*
Knit 3 rows.
Row 26: [K2tog] twice. *(2 sts)*
Row 27: K2tog and fasten off.

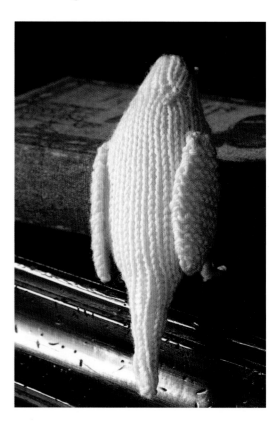

WINGS
To keep the wings flat, pin them down using a little stitch.

To Make Up

SEWING IN ENDS Sew in ends, leaving ends from cast on and cast (bound) off rows for sewing up.

BODY With RS together, fold the body in half. Using mattress or whip stitch, sew up tail and around the bottom edge of body to head, leaving a 2.5cm (1in) gap at tummy. Turn RS out.

TAIL Cut a pipecleaner 2.5cm (1in) longer than the tail. Fold over one end. Slip the folded end into the tail, add a little stuffing. The end of the pipecleaner will poke out and will vanish into the body stuffing.

STUFFING Starting at the head, stuff the body and. Sew up the gap.

WINGS Sew cast (bound) off row of wing to body, with the longer curve at the bottom of the wing. To stop the wings flapping, halfway down wing sew the underside of wing to the body with a little stitch.

LEGS AND FEET Cut a 12.5cm (5in) length of pipecleaner. Thread the pipecleaner through bottom edge of the tummy, leaving 1cm (½in) between the two legs. The legs should be about 2.5cm (1in) long. To make feet, fold the pipecleaner back on itself twice and trim. Repeat for other foot. Using sh and starting at the feet, wrap the feet and legs in yarn. Secure at top of legs.

BEAK Cut 2.5cm (1in) of pipecleaner. With sh, wrap 2cm (¾in) of pipecleaner, do not cut off yarn, fold in half and push into the head. Use the ends of the yarn to secure the beak.

EYES With bl, sew 3-loop French knots, positioned as in photograph.

LEGS
A little pink nail varnish on the claws will prevent the yarn unravelling.

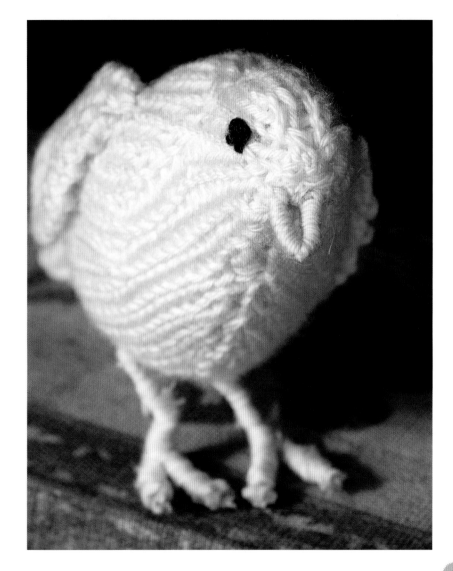

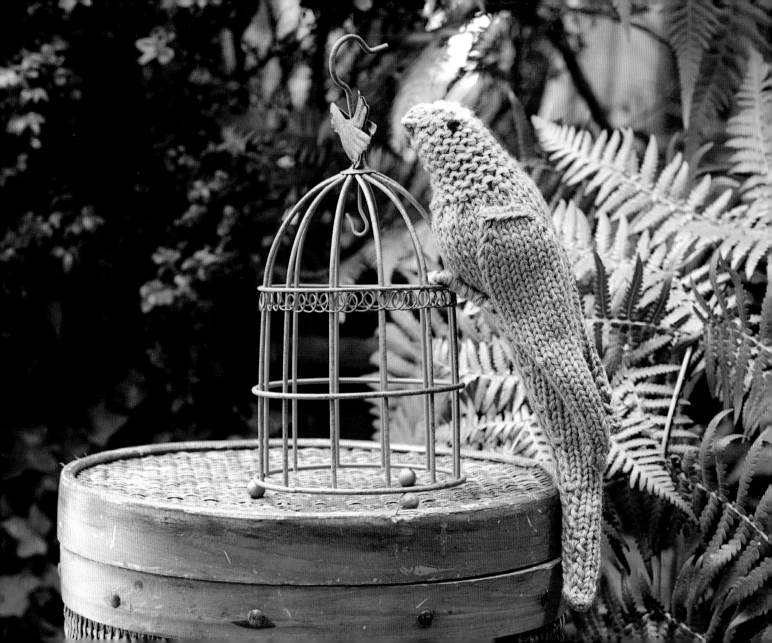

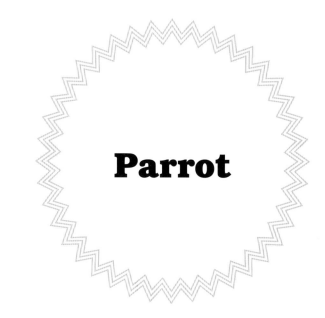

Parrot

Parrots are one of the most intelligent species of bird, and can imitate human speech. Parrots will eat anything, but chocolate is poisonous to them. If looked after well a parrot will live as long as you, so be prepared to have a pet for your whole life – or you could knit one. Although parrots are very colourful, their eggs are always white. The most famous parrot is Captain Flint, who sits on Long John Silver's shoulder in *Treasure Island*.

Parrot

The parrot needs to be stuffed firmly.

Measurements

Length from beak to tail: 27cm (10½in)

Materials

Pair of 3¼mm (US 3) knitting needles
40g (1½oz) of Rowan Pure Wool DK in
Avocado 019 (av) used DOUBLE throughout
5g (⅙oz) of Rowan Pure Wool DK in Gold 051
(go) used DOUBLE throughout
5g (⅙oz) of Rowan Pure Wool DK in Clay 048
(cl) used DOUBLE throughout
Tiny amount of Rowan Pure Wool DK in
Black 004 (bl) for eyes
Pipecleaner for claws.

Abbreviations

See page 12.

Body

With av, cast on 7 sts.
Beg with a k row, work 10 rows st st.
Row 11: K1, inc, k3, inc, k1. *(9 sts)*
Work 7 rows st st.
Row 19: K1, inc, k5, inc, k1. *(11 sts)*
Work 7 rows st st.
Row 27: K1, inc, k7, inc, k1. *(13 sts)*
Work 5 rows st st.
Row 33: K1, inc, k9, inc, k1. *(15 sts)*
Work 5 rows st st.
Row 39: K1, inc, k11, inc, k1. *(17 sts)*
Work 5 rows st st.
Row 45: K1, inc, k13, inc, k1. *(19 sts)*
Work 5 rows st st.
Row 51: K1, inc, k15, inc, k1. *(21 sts)*

Row 52: Purl.
Row 53: K1, inc, k4, inc, k7, inc, k4, inc, k1.
(25 sts)
Row 54: Purl.
Row 55: K1, inc, k5, inc, k9, inc, k5, inc, k1.
(29 sts)
Row 56: Purl.
Row 57: K1, inc, k25, inc, k1. *(31 sts)*
Row 58: Purl.
Row 59: K1, inc, k6, inc, k13, inc, k6, inc, k1.
(35 sts)
Row 60: Purl.
Work 6 rows st st.

Shape head

Row 67: [K2tog, k1] 11 times, k2tog. *(23 sts)*
Work 1 row garter st.
Row 69: [K2tog, k2] twice, k2tog, k3, k2tog,
[k2, k2tog] twice. *(17 sts)*
Work 8 rows garter st.
Join in go.
Row 78: K6av, k5go, k6av.
Rep row 78, 4 more times.
Row 83: [K2togav] 3 times, k2toggo, k1go,
k2toggo, [k2togav] 3 times. *(9 sts)*
Row 84: K2togav, k1av, k3toggo, k1av,
k2togav. *(5 sts)*
Cont in cl.
Row 85: K2tog, k1, k2tog. *(3 sts)*
Work 4 rows st st.
Row 90: P2tog, p1. *(2 sts)*
Row 91: K2tog and fasten off.

Wing

(make 2 the same)
With av, cast on 2 sts.
Beg with a k row, work 2 rows st st.
Row 3: [Inc] twice. *(4 sts)*
Row 4: Purl.
Work 2 rows st st.
Row 7: Inc, k2, inc. *(6 sts)*
Work 3 rows st st.
Row 11: Inc, k4, inc. *(8 sts)*
Work 3 rows st st.
Row 15: Inc, k6, inc. *(10 sts)*
Work 23 rows st st.
Row 39: K2tog, k6, k2tog. *(8 sts)*
Row 40: Purl.
Row 41: K2tog, k4, k2tog. *(6 sts)*
Row 42: Purl.
Cast (bind) off.

FEET

The parrot is made to perch on
the edge of something.

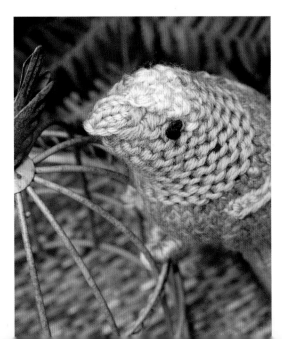

To Make Up

SEWING IN ENDS Sew in ends, leaving ends from cast on and cast (bound) off rows for sewing up.

BODY AND STUFFING With RS together and starting at tail, sew up leaving 2.5cm (1in) gap. Stuff firmly and sew up gap.

WINGS Sew wings on at diagonal, starting where garter st for head begins; sew them down for 6cm (2½in).

EYES With bl, sew 4-loop French knots positioned as in photograph.

BEAK Sew tip of beak down with 1 stitch.

CLAWS Thread pipecleaner through body approx 15cm (6in) from tail end, leaving 3 sts either side of centre seam between where it goes in and comes out. Fold each end of pipecleaner into a Y-shape, winding it back on itself. Wrap claws in 2 ends of cl. Bend into shape.

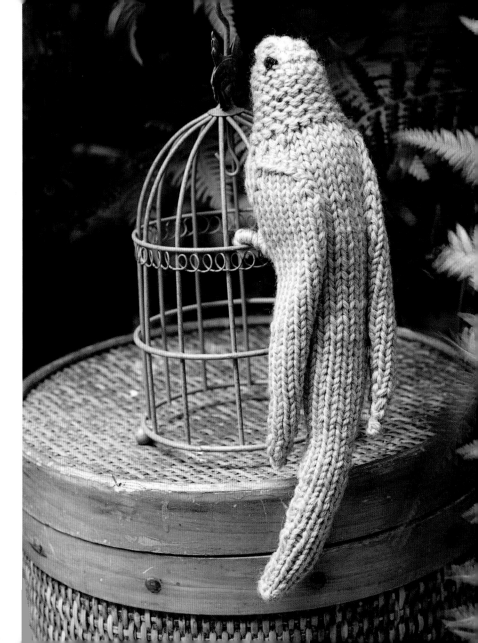

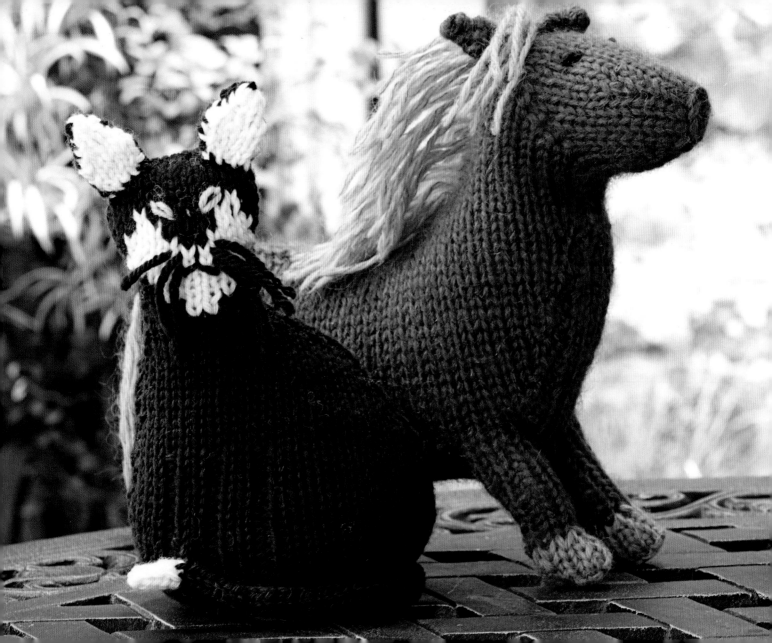

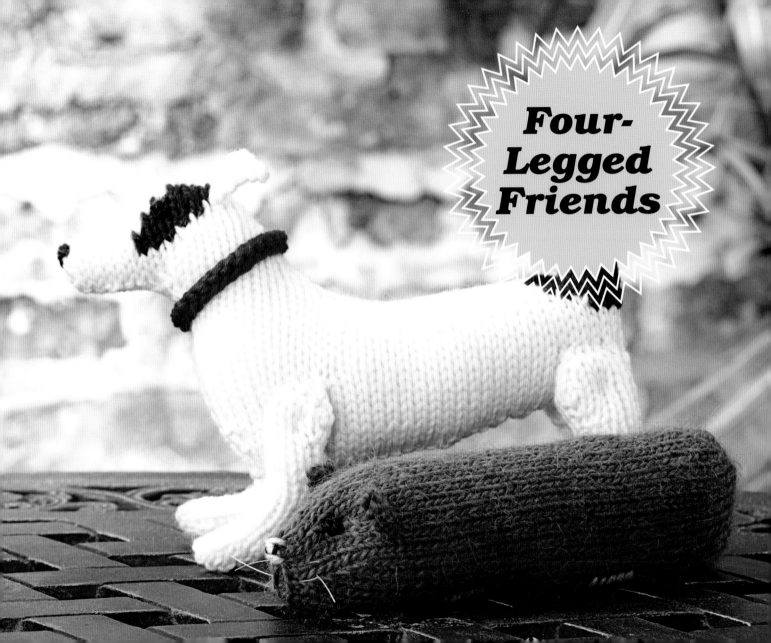

Four-Legged Friends

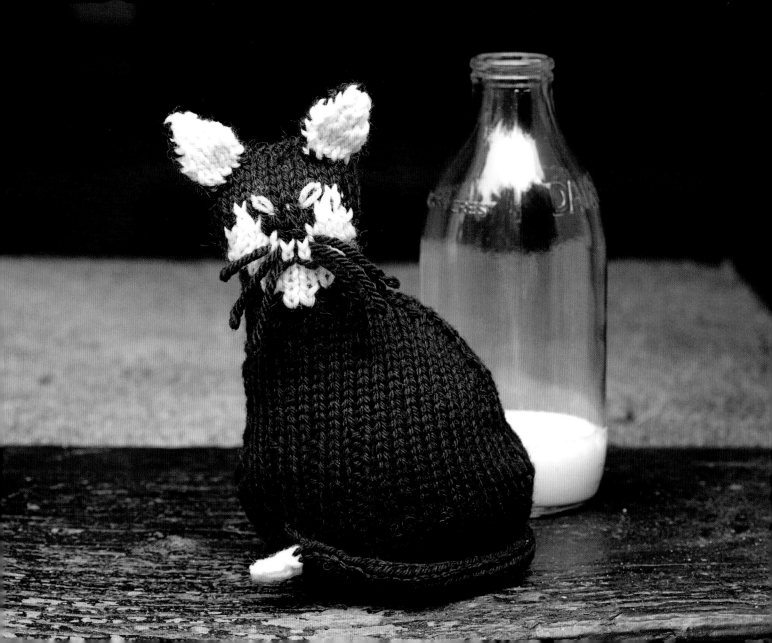

Simple Cat

The most popular pet, cats are independent and yet excellent companions with strong opinions. Cats are good hunters, liable to bring you a present of a dead bird, but will also keep the mouse population in your house in check. Ours is a black and white cat, but you can use whatever colours you want to create your own puss.

Simple Cat

An easy-to-knit sitting cat who is a good introduction to knitting our other cats.

Measurements
Width: 13cm (5in)
Height to top of ears: 22cm (9in)

Materials
Pair of 3¼mm (US 3) knitting needles
40g (1½oz) of Rowan Pure Wool Aran in Noir 685 (nr)
5g (⅙oz) of Rowan Pure Wool Aran in Ivory 670 (iv)
Tiny amount of Rowan Pure Wool 4ply in Gerbera 454 (ga) for eyes
Rice or lentils with small plastic bag for stuffing (optional)
Crochet hook

Abbreviations
See page 12.
See page 13 for Colour Knitting.

Back
With nr, cast on 20 sts.
Beg with a k row, work 2 rows st st.
Row 3: Inc, k4, inc, k8, inc, k4, inc. *(24 sts)*
Work 3 rows st st.
Row 7: Inc, k5, inc, k10, inc, k5, inc. *(28 sts)*
Work 5 rows st st.
Row 13: Inc, k25, k2tog. *(28 sts)*
Work 3 rows st st.
Row 17: K2tog, k24, k2tog. *(26 sts)*
Row 18: Purl.
Row 19: K24, k2tog. *(25 sts)*
Row 20: Purl.
Row 21: K2tog, k21, k2tog. *(23 sts)*
Row 22: Purl.
Row 23: K21, k2tog. *(22 sts)*
Row 24: Purl.
Row 25: K20, k2tog. *(21 sts)*
Row 26: Purl.
Row 27: K2tog, k17, k2tog. *(19 sts)*
Row 28: P2tog, p17. *(18 sts)*
Row 29: K16, k2tog. *(17 sts)*
Row 30: P2tog, p15. *(16 sts)*
Row 31: K2tog, k12, k2tog. *(14 sts)*
Row 32: Cast (bind) off 2 sts, p to end. *(12 sts)*

Row 33: Knit.
Row 34: Cast (bind) off 2 sts, p to end. *(10 sts)*
Work 2 rows st st.
Row 37: K2tog, k6, k2tog. *(8 sts)*
Work 3 rows st st.
Row 41: Inc, k6, inc. *(10 sts)*
Row 42: Inc, p8, inc. *(12 sts)*
Row 43: Knit.
Row 44: Inc, p10, inc. *(14 sts)*
Work 5 rows st st.
Row 50: P2tog, p10, p2tog. *(12 sts)*
Row 51: K2tog, k8, k2tog. *(10 sts)*
Cast (bind) off.

Front
With nr, cast on 20 sts.
Row 1: K11, p1, k2, p1, k2, p1, k2.
Row 2: P2, k1, p2, k1, p2, k1, p11.
Row 3: Inc, k10, p1, k2, p1, k2, p1, k1, inc. *(22 sts)*
Row 4: P3, k1, p2, k1, p2, k1, p12.
Row 5: K12, p1, k2, p1, k2, p1, k3.
Row 6: P3, k1, p2, k1, p2, k1, p12.
Row 7: Inc, k11, p1, k2, p1, k2, p1, k2, inc. *(24 sts)*
Row 8: P4, k1, p2, k1, p2, k1, p13.
Row 9: K13, p1, k2, p1, k2, p1, k4.
Row 10: P4, k1, p2, k1, p2, k1, p13.
Row 11: K13, p1, k2, p1, k2, p1, k4.
Row 12: P4, k1, p2, k1, p2, k1, p13.
Row 13: K2tog, k11, p1, k2, p1, k2, p1, k3, inc. *(24 sts)*
Row 14: P5, k1, p2, k1, p2, k1, p12.
Row 15: K12, p1, k2, p1, k2, p1, k5.
Row 16: P5, k1, p2, k1, p2, k1, p12.
Row 17: K2tog, k10, p1, k2, p1, k2, p1, k3, k2tog. *(22 sts)*
Row 18: P4, k1, p2, k1, p2, k1, p11.
Row 19: K11, p1, k2, p1, k2, p1, k4.
Row 20: Purl.
Row 21: K2tog, k20. *(21 sts)*
Row 22: Purl.
Row 23: Knit.

Give this cat some stripes and he becomes a cute tabby cat.

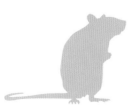

TAIL

The tail can be any length,
just add more rows.

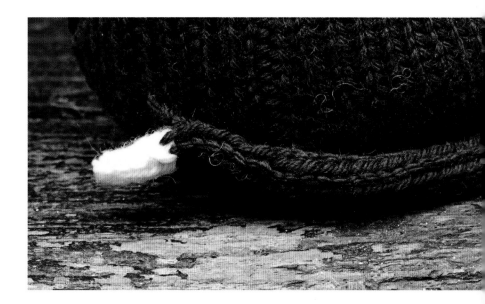

Row 24: P2tog, p17, p2tog. *(19 sts)*
Row 25: Knit.
Row 26: Purl.
Row 27: K2tog, k17. *(18 sts)*
Row 28: Purl.
Row 29: K2tog, k16. *(17 sts)*
Row 30: P15, p2tog. *(16 sts)*
Row 31: K2tog, k12, k2tog. (14 sts)
Row 32: Purl.
Row 33: Cast (bind) off 2 sts, k to end.
(12 sts)
Row 34: Purl.
Row 35: Cast (bind) off 2 sts, k to end.
(10 sts)
Join in iv.
Row 36: P4nr, p2iv, p4nr.
Row 37: K2tognr, k2nr, k2iv, k2nr, k2tognr.
(8 sts)
Row 38: P2nr, p4iv, p2nr.

Row 39: K2nr, k4iv, k2nr.
Row 40: P1nr, p6iv, p1nr.
Row 41: Inciv, k6iv, inciv. *(10 sts)*
Row 42: Inciv, p8iv, inciv. *(12 sts)*
Row 43: K1nr, k4iv, k2nr, k4iv, k1nr.
Row 44: Incnr, p3iv, p4nr, p3iv, incnr.
(14 sts)
Row 45: K3nr, k2iv, k4nr, k2iv, k3nr.
Row 46: P3nr, p1iv, p6nr, p1iv, p3nr.
Cont in nr.
Work 3 rows st st.
Row 50: P2tog, p10, p2tog. *(12 sts)*
Row 51: K2tog, k8, k2tog. *(10 sts)*
Cast (bind) off.

Bottom

With nr, cast on 8 sts.
Beg with a k row, work 2 rows st st.
Row 3: Inc, k6, inc. *(10 sts)*
Row 4: Purl.
Row 5: Inc, k8, inc. *(12 sts)*
Row 6: Purl.
Row 7: Inc, k10, inc. *(14 sts)*
Work 7 rows st st.
Row 15: K2tog, k10, k2tog. *(12 sts)*
Row 16: Purl
Row 17: K2tog, k8, k2tog. *(10 sts)*
Row 18: Purl.
Row 19: K2tog, k6, k2tog. *(8 sts)*
Row 20: Purl.
Cast (bind) off.

Tail

With nr, cast on 6 sts.
Beg with a k row, work 22 rows st st.
Row 23: K2tog, k2, k2tog. *(4 sts)*
Work 7 rows st st.
Cont in iv.
Work 4 rows st st.

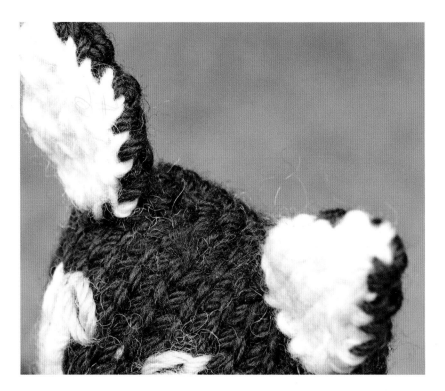

EARS
The ears can also be single thickness and all black.

Row 35: [K2tog] twice. *(2 sts)*
Row 36: P2tog and fasten off.

Ear

(make 4 the same, 2 in nr and 2 in iv)
With nr/iv, cast on 5 sts.
Beg with a k row, work 4 rows st st.
Row 5: K2tog, k1, k2tog. *(3 sts)*
Row 6: Purl.
Row 7: K3tog and fasten off.

To Make Up

SEWING IN ENDS Sew in ends, leaving ends from cast on row and cast (bound) off rows for sewing up.
HEAD AND BODY With WS together, sew around the body and head.
BOTTOM With WS together, attach the bottom to the base of the cat, leaving a 2.5cm (1in) gap.
STUFFING Starting at the head, stuff the cat firmly. To help the cat sit properly, fill a small plastic bag with rice or lentils and stuff into the bottom of the cat. Sew up the gap. Mould into shape.
TAIL Fold over tail and sew together on RS side. Attach to right side at base of cat. With a small stitch attach the tip of the tail to centre of body.
EARS With WS together in bl, sew the front and back of the ears together. Sew cast on row of ear to head, with 2cm (¾in) between ears.
EYES With ga, sew 2 chain stitch eyes, positioned as in photograph.
MOUTH With bl, embroider one vertical and two horizontal lines in satin stitch.
WHISKERS: With bl, cut 8cm (3in) lengths and with a crochet hook slip through the face, either side of the vertical line for mouth, leaving two stitches in the centre.

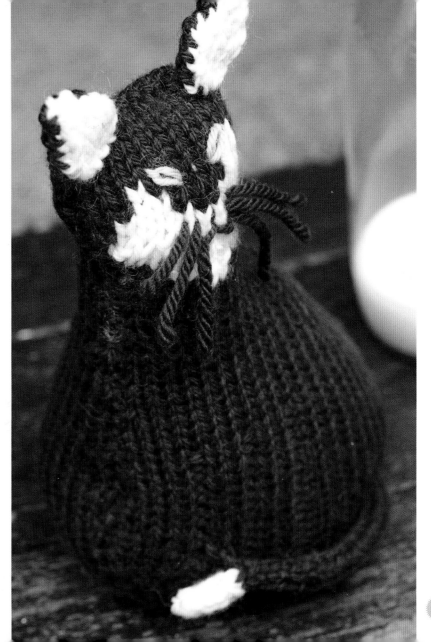

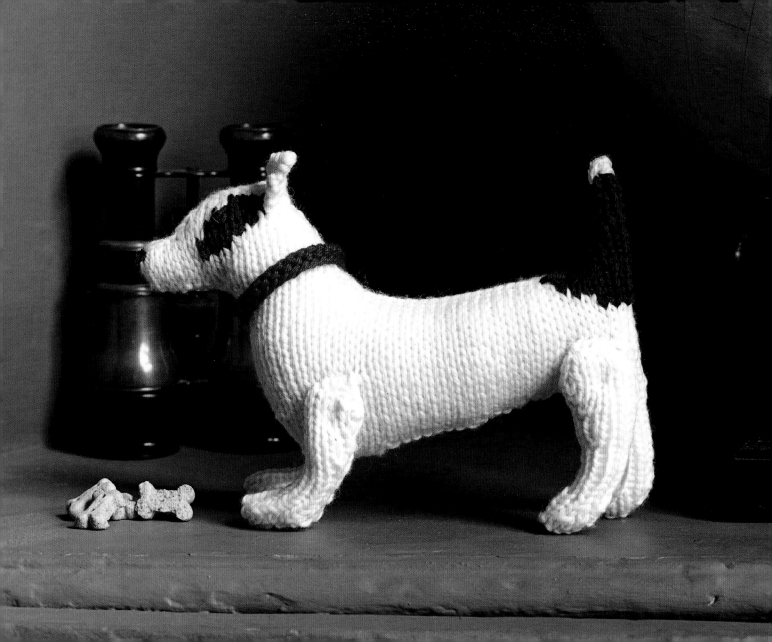

Simple Dog

Related to the wolf, dogs are popular pets worldwide. For years dogs were considered to be either working animals or lap dogs, but over the past few decades the dog has become an important member of the family, treated almost like a child. Owners talk to them and love their companionship; and they now work helping people with medical problems: hearing dogs, seeing dogs and even dogs that detect early signs of an epileptic fit. Ours is a standard terrier-type.

Simple Dog

Introducing you to knitting dogs; once completed you will be able to knit most of the dogs from our other *Best In Show* books.

Measurements
Length: 23cm (9in)
Height to top of head: 17cm (6¾in)

Materials
Pair of 3¼mm (US 3) knitting needles
Double-pointed 3¼mm (US 3) knitting needles (for holding stitches)
30g (1¼oz) of Rowan Pure Wool Aran in Ivory 670 (iv)
5g (⅛oz) of Rowan Pure Wool DK in Earth 018 (eh) used DOUBLE throughout
2 pipecleaners for legs
Tiny amount of Rowan Pure Wool 4ply in Black 404 (bl) for nose and eyes
Small amount of Rowan Pure Wool Aran in Ember 679 (em) for collar (optional)

Abbreviations
See page 12.
See page 13 for Colour Knitting.

Back Leg
(make 2 the same)
With iv, cast on 9 sts.
Work 2 rows st st.
Row 3: Inc, k1, k2tog, k1, k2tog, k1, inc. *(9 sts)*
Row 4: Purl.
Row 5: Inc, k1, k2tog, k1, k2tog, k1, inc. *(9 sts)*
Row 6: Purl.
Row 7: K2tog, k5, k2tog. *(7 sts)**
Work 5 rows st st.
Row 13: K2, inc, k1, inc, k2. *(9 sts)*
Work 3 rows st st.
Row 17: K3, inc, k1, inc, k3. *(11 sts)*
Row 18: Purl.
Row 19: K4, inc, k1, inc, k4. *(13 sts)*
Row 20: Purl.
Row 21: K5, inc, k1, inc, k5. *(15 sts)*
Row 22: Purl.
Row 23: K5, k2tog, k1, k2tog, k5. *(13 sts)*
Row 24: Purl.
Cast (bind) off.

Front Leg
(make 2 the same)
Work as for Back Leg to *.
Work 7 rows st st.
Row 15: Inc, k5, inc. (9 sts)
Work 3 rows st st.
Row 19: Inc, k7, inc. (11 sts)
Row 20: Purl.
Row 21: K2tog, k7, k2tog. (9 sts)
Row 22: Purl.
Cast (bind) off.

Right Side of Body
With iv, cast on 10 sts.
Row 1: K10, cast on 8 sts. *(18 sts)*
Row 2: Purl.
Row 3: Inc, k17, cast on 4 sts. *(23 sts)*
Row 4: Purl.
Row 5: Inc, k22, cast on 10 sts. *(34 sts)*
Work 10 rows st st.
Join in eh.

Row 16: P4eh, p30iv.
Row 17: K28iv, k6eh.
Row 18: P7eh, p27iv.
Row 19: K27iv, k7eh.
Row 20: P5eh (hold 5 sts on spare needle for Tail), cast (bind) off 2 sts eh, 17 sts iv, p10iv icos.
Working on 10 sts for neck and head only, cont in iv.
Work 2 rows st st.
Row 23: Inc, k7, k2tog. *(10 sts)*
Row 24: Purl.
Row 25: Inc, k9. *(11 sts)*
Row 26: P11, cast on 7 sts. *(18 sts)*
Row 27: K16, k2tog. *(17 sts)*
Work 2 rows st st.
Row 30: P2tog, p15. *(16 sts)*
Work 2 rows st st.
Row 33: Cast (bind) off 4 sts, k to end. *(12 sts)*
Row 34: Purl.
Row 35: K2tog, k8, k2tog. *(10 sts)*
Row 36: P8, p2tog. *(9 sts)*
Row 37: Knit.
Row 38: Purl.
Row 39: K2tog, k5, k2tog. *(7 sts)*
Row 40: P2tog, p3, p2tog. *(5 sts)*
Cast (bind) off.

Left Side of Body
With iv, cast on 10 sts.
Row 1: P10, cast on 8 sts. *(18 sts)*
Row 2: Knit.
Row 3: Inc, p17, cast on 4 sts. *(23 sts)*
Row 4: Knit.
Row 5: Inc, p22, cast on 10 sts. *(34 sts)*
Work 10 rows st st.
Join in eh.
Row 16: K4eh, k30iv.
Row 17: P28iv, p6eh.
Row 18: K7eh, k27iv.
Row 19: P27iv, p7eh.
Row 20: K5eh (hold 5 sts on spare needle for Tail), cast (bind) off 2 sts eh, 17 sts iv, k10iv icos.

PIPECLEANERS

For young children, this stocky dog
can be made without pipecleaners.

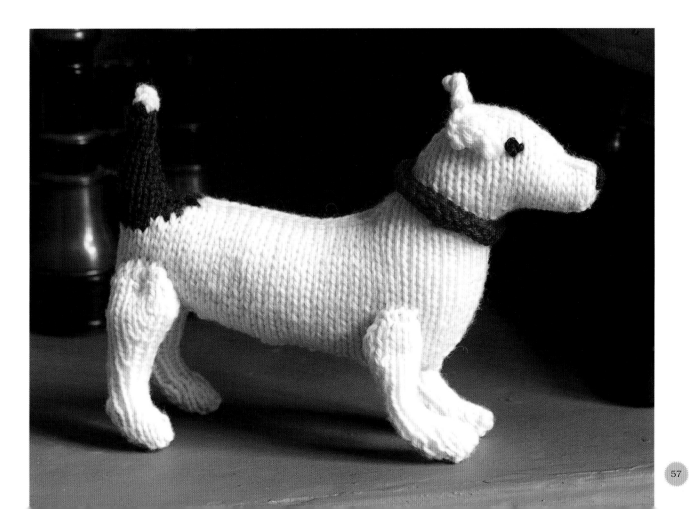

Working on 10 sts for neck and head only, cont in iv.

Work 2 rows st st.

Row 23: Inc, p7, p2tog. *(10 sts)*

Row 24: Knit.

Row 25: Inc, p9. *(11 sts)*

Row 26: K11, cast on 7 sts. *(18 sts)*

Row 27: P16, p2tog. *(17 sts)*

Row 28: Knit.

Join in eh.

Row 29: P7iv, p3eh, p7iv.

Row 30: K2togiv, k4iv, k4eh, k7iv. *(16 sts)*

Row 31: P6iv, p1ch, p5iv.

Row 32: K5iv, k5ch, k6iv.

Row 33: Cast (bind) off 4iv, p1iv, p5ch, p5iv. *(12 sts)*

Row 34: K5iv, k4ch, k5iv.

Row 35: P2togiv, p4ch, p3iv, p2togiv. *(10 sts)*

Row 36: K4iv, k4ch, k2togiv. *(9 sts)*

Cont in iv.

Work 2 rows st st.

Row 39: P2tog, p5, p2tog. *(7 sts)*

Row 40: K2tog, k3, k2tog. *(5 sts)*

Cast (bind) off.

Tail

Row 1: With eh and with RS facing, k5 from spare needle of Left Side of Body then k5 from spare needle of Right Side of Body. *(10 sts)*

Row 2: Purl.

Row 3: K3, [k2tog] twice, k3. *(8 sts)*

Work 3 rows st st.

Row 7: K2, [k2tog] twice, k2. *(6 sts)*

Work 3 rows st st.

Row 11: K1, [k2tog] twice, k1. *(4 sts)*

Cont in iv.

Row 12: Purl.

Row 13: [K2tog] twice. *(2 sts)*

Row 14: P2tog and fasten off.

Right Ear

With iv, cast on 5 sts.

Knit 3 rows.

Row 4: Purl.

Row 5: Knit.

Row 6: P2tog, p1, p2tog. *(3 sts)*

Row 7: Knit.

Row 8: Purl.

Row 9: Knit.

Row 10: P3tog and fasten off.

Left Ear

With iv, cast on 5 sts.

Knit 5 rows.

Row 6: K2tog, k1, k2tog. *(3 sts)*

Knit 3 rows.

Row 10: K3tog and fasten off.

Collar

(optional)

With em, cast on 28 sts.

Knit one row.

Cast (bind) off.

LEGS

To help the dog stand upright, make a stitch from one leg, through the body to the other leg and secure firmly.

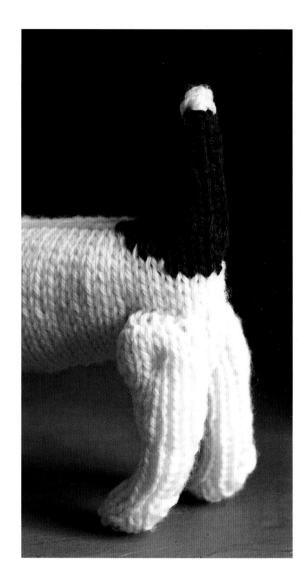

To Make Up

SEWING IN ENDS Sew in ends, leaving ends from cast on row and cast (bound) off rows for sewing up.

LEGS With WS together, fold leg in half. Starting at the paw, sew up legs on RS. Cut a pipecleaner to approximately fit the leg, leaving an extra 2.5cm (1in); fold over both ends. Roll a little stuffing around the pipecleaner and slip into leg. Push stuffing down to the paw and fill. Sew across the top. Leave an end for sewing leg onto body.

HEAD, BODY AND TAIL Sew around head, body and tail, leaving a 2.5cm (1in) gap at the tummy.

STUFFING Starting at the head, stuff the dog firmly, pushing a little into the tail, then sew up gap. Mould into shape.

EARS Sew cast on row of ear to head, with 1cm (½in) between ears. Fold over right ear and sew tip to head.

EYES With bl, sew 3-loop French knots, positioned as in photograph.

NOSE With bl, embroider the nose in satin stitch.

COLLAR Sew ends of collar together and pop over head.

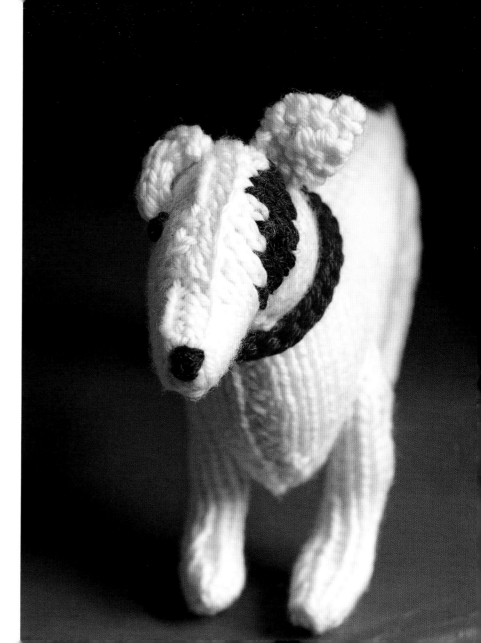

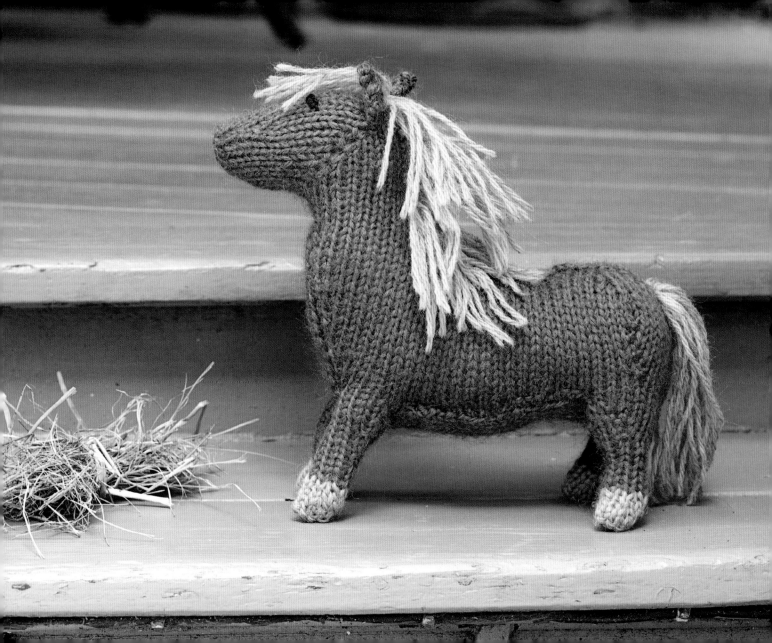

Shetland Pony

A little workhorse, the Shetland pony really does originate from the Shetland Isles. They are strong, small and intelligent, and used to work down the mines as pit ponies and on farms pulling carts. These days they are more likely to be ridden by children or harnessed to a carriage for competing at shows. We had one, called Starlight, an utterly fiendish and unapproachable pony, but we loved her all the same. The English cartoonist, Norman Thelwell, wrote many books featuring an impish, big-bottomed Shetland pony called Kipper.

Shetland Pony

The tail and mane need to be luxurious.

Measurements
Length: 25cm (10in)
Height to top of head: 22cm (8¾in)

Materials
Pair of 4mm (US 6) knitting needles
Double-pointed 4mm (US 6) knitting needles
(for holding stitches)
10g (¼oz) of Rowan Kid Classic in Mellow
877 (ml) used DOUBLE throughout
55g (2oz) of Rowan Kid Classic in Bear 817
(be) used DOUBLE throughout
2 pipecleaners
Tiny amount of Rowan Pure Wool 4ply in
Black 404 (bl) for eyes

Abbreviations
See page 12.
See page 13 for Scarf Fringe Method.
See page 13 for Wrap and Turn Method.

Right Back Leg
With ml, cast on 9 sts.
Beg with k row, work 2 rows st st.
Row 3: Inc, k1, k2tog, k1, k2tog, k1, inc.
(9 sts)
Row 4: Purl.
Cont in be.
Row 5: K2, k2tog, k1, k2tog, k2. *(7 sts)*
Work 7 rows st st.*
Row 13: K2, inc, k1, inc, k2. *(9 sts)*
Row 14: Purl.
Row 15: K3, inc, k1, inc, k3. *(11 sts)*
Row 16: Purl.
Row 17: K4, inc, k1, inc, k4. *(13 sts)*
Row 18: Purl.**
Row 19: Cast (bind) off 6 sts, k to end (hold
7 sts on spare needle for Right Side of Body).

Left Back Leg
Work as for Right Back Leg to **.
Row 19: K7, cast (bind) off 6 sts (hold 7 sts
on spare needle for Left Side of Body).

Right Front Leg
Work as for Right Back Leg to *.
Row 13: Inc, k5, inc. *(9 sts)*
Work 3 rows st st.***

Row 17: Cast (bind) off 4 sts, k to end
(hold 5 sts on spare needle for Right Side
of Body).

Left Front Leg
Work as for Right Front Leg to ***.
Row 17: K5, cast (bind) off 4 sts (hold 5 sts
on spare needle for Left Side of Body).

Right Side of Body
Row 1: With be, cast on 1 st, k5 from
spare needle of Right Front Leg, cast on
8 sts. *(14 sts)*
Row 2: Purl.
Row 3: Inc, k13, cast on 4 sts. *(19 sts)*
Row 4: Purl.
Row 5: Inc, k18, cast on 2 sts, k7 from
spare needle of Right Back Leg, cast on
2 sts. *(31 sts)*
Row 6: Purl.
Row 7: K25, inc, k5. *(32 sts)*
Row 8: Purl.
Row 9: Inc, k24, inc, k6. *(34 sts)*
Row 10: Purl.
Row 11: K26, inc, k7. *(35 sts)*
Row 12: Purl.
Row 13: Inc, k26, inc, k7. *(37 sts)*
Work 3 rows st st.
Row 17: K28, k2tog, k5, k2tog. *(35 sts)*
Row 18: P2tog, p33. *(34 sts)*
Row 19: Inc, k25, k2tog, k4, k2tog. *(33 sts)*
Row 20: P2tog, p8, p2tog, cast (bind) off
8 sts, p to end (hold 13 sts on spare needle
for right side of neck).
Row 21: Rejoin yarn, k2tog, k2, k2tog, k2,
k2tog. *(7 sts)*
Cast (bind) off.

The pony's curvy shape means it needs lots of stuffing.

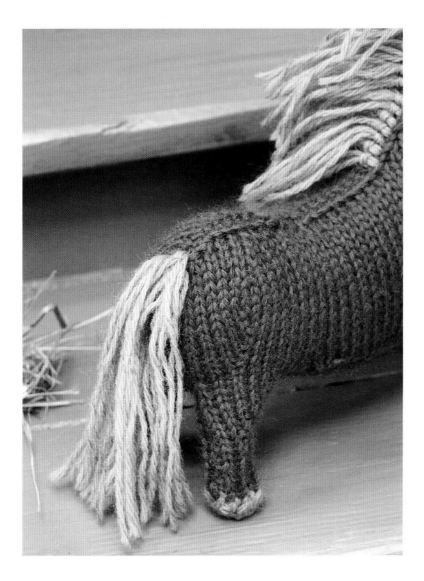

RUMP
Stuff the pony's bottom well to give it that characteristic big rump.

Left Side of Body
Row 1: With be, cast on 1 st, p5 from spare needle of Left Front Leg, cast on 8 sts. *(14 sts)*
Row 2: Knit.
Row 3: Inc, p13, cast on 4 sts. *(19 sts)*
Row 4: Knit.
Row 5: Inc, p18, cast on 2 sts, p7 from spare needle of Left Back Leg, cast on 2 sts. *(31 sts)*
Row 6: Knit.
Row 7: P25, inc, p5. *(32 sts)*
Row 8: Knit.
Row 9: Inc, p24, inc, p6. *(34 sts)*
Row 10: Knit.
Row 11: P26, inc, p7. *(35 sts)*
Row 12: Knit.
Row 13: Inc, p26, inc, p7. *(37 sts)*
Work 3 rows st st.
Row 17: P28, p2tog, p5, p2tog. *(35 sts)*
Row 18: K2tog, k33. *(34 sts)*
Row 19: Inc, p25, p2tog, p4, p2tog. *(33 sts)*
Row 20: K2tog, k8, k2tog, cast (bind) off 8 sts, k to end (hold 13 sts on spare needle for left side of neck).
Row 21: Rejoin yarn, p2tog, p2, p2tog, p2, p2tog. *(7 sts)*
Cast (bind) off.

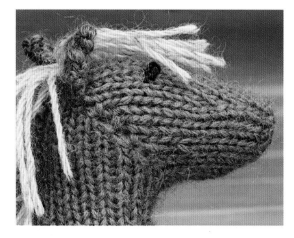

FORELOCK
To make a forelock, take some of the mane between the ears.

Neck and Head
Row 1: With be and RS facing, k11, k2tog from spare needle of Right Side of Body and k2tog, k11 from spare needle of Left Side of Body. *(24 sts)*
Row 2: Purl.
Row 3: Inc, k9, [k2tog] twice, k9, inc. *(24 sts)*
Row 4: Purl.
Row 5: K10, [k2tog] twice, k10. *(22 sts)*
Row 6: Purl.
Row 7: Inc, k8, [k2tog] twice, k8, inc. *(22 sts)*
Row 8: Purl.
Row 9: K18, wrap and turn (leave 4 sts on spare needle).
Row 10: P14, w&t.
Row 11: K13, w&t.
Row 12: P12, w&t.
Row 13: K11, w&t.
Row 14: P10, w&t.
Row 15: K9, w&t.
Row 16: P8, w&t.
Row 17: K7, w&t.
Row 18: P6, w&t.

Row 19: K7, w&t.
Row 20: P8, w&t.
Row 21: K9, w&t.
Row 22: P10, w&t.
Row 23: K11, w&t.
Row 24: P12, w&t.
Row 25: K13, w&t.
Row 26: P14, w&t.
Row 27: K18. *(22 sts in total)*
Work 3 rows st st.
Row 31: K6, k2tog, k6, k2tog, k6. *(20 sts)*
Row 32: Purl.
Row 33: K2tog, k4, k2tog, k4, k2tog, k4, k2tog. *(16 sts)*
Row 34: Purl.
Row 35: K2tog, k3, k2tog, k2, k2tog, k3, k2tog. *(12 sts)*
Row 36: Purl.
Row 37: K2tog, k8, k2tog. *(10 sts)*
Cast (bind) off.

Tummy
With be, cast on 7 sts.
Beg with a k row, work 14 rows st st.

Row 15: Inc, k5, inc. *(9 sts)*
Work 15 rows st st.
Row 31: K2tog, k5, k2tog. *(7 sts)*
Work 9 rows st st.
Row 41: K2tog, k3, k2tog. *(5 sts)*
Work 17 rows st st.
Row 59: K2tog, k1, k2tog. *(3 sts)*
Work 3 rows st st.
Row 63: K3tog and fasten off.

Ear
(make 2 the same)
With be, cast on 4 sts.
Knit 4 rows.
Row 5: [K2tog] twice. *(2 sts)*
Knit 2 rows.
Row 8: K2tog and fasten off.

To Make Up
SEWING IN ENDS Sew in ends, leaving ends from cast on row and cast (bound) off rows for sewing up.
LEGS With WS together, fold leg in half. Starting at hoof, sew up legs on RS.

BODY Sew along back of pony and around its bottom.

TUMMY Sew cast on row of tummy to bottom of pony's bottom (where legs begin), and sew cast (bound) off row to just below neck. Ease and sew tummy to fit body, matching curves of tummy to legs. Leave a 2.5cm (1in) gap between front and back legs on one side.

HEAD AND NOSE Fold in half and sew together to top of tummy.

STUFFING Pipecleaners are used to stiffen the legs and help bend them into shape. Fold a pipecleaner into a U-shape and measure against front two legs. Cut to fit approximately, leaving an extra 2.5cm (1in) at both ends. Fold these ends over to stop the pipecleaner poking out of the hooves. Roll a little stuffing around the pipecleaner and slip into body, one end down each front leg. Repeat with second pipecleaner and back legs. Starting at the head, stuff the pony firmly, especially at the bottom, then sew up the gap. Mould body into shape.

TAIL With ml, cut 14 x 20cm (8in) lengths of yarn, fold in half; with another length, knot the yarn together at the fold. Attach tail to start of bottom. Trim.

EARS Sew cast on row of each ear to head, with 3 stitches between ears.

EYES With bl, sew 3 slanting satin stitches, positioned as in photograph.

MANE: Cut approx 34 x 15cm (6in) lengths of ml. Use crochet hook and scarf fringe method to attach pairs of strands in tufts along the centre of the neck and between the ears. Trim to shape as in photograph: the Shetland pony has a shaggy feel.

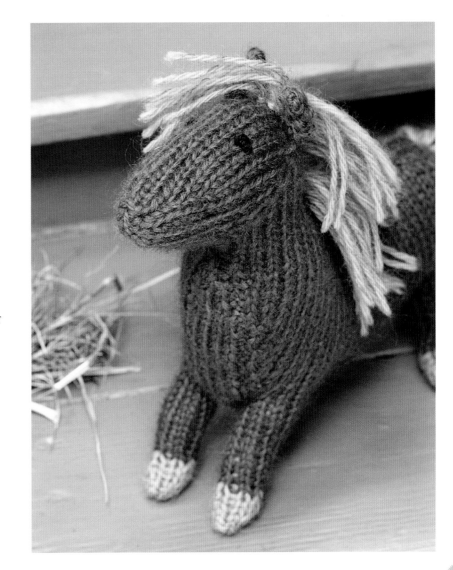

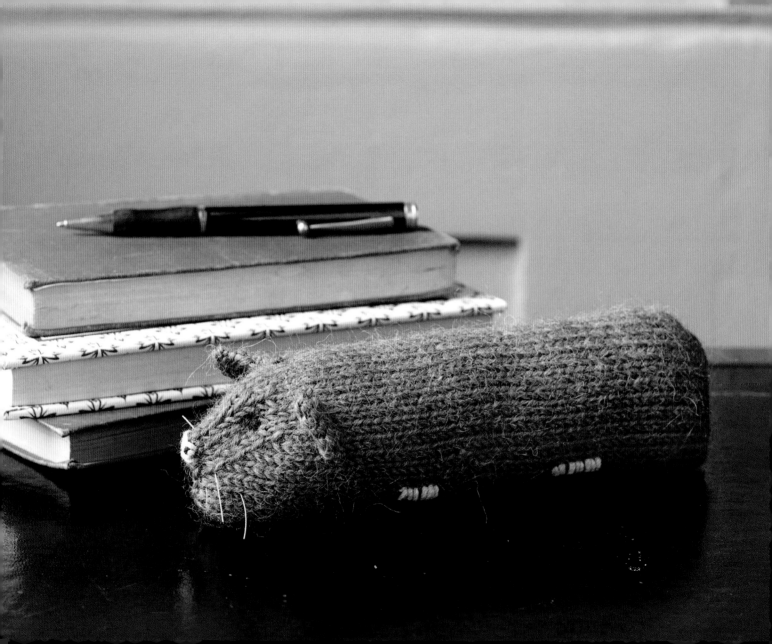

Guinea Pig

Guinea pigs come from South America, where they are a delicacy. They like to live in large groups, called herds. Baby guinea pigs, known as pups, are born with hair, open eyes and all their teeth. Guinea pigs make delightful pets, being friendly and talkative; they squeak, purr and popcorn - which means jumping up and down with excitement. Michael Bond, who wrote the Paddington Bear books, also wrote about a guinea pig called Olga da Polga.

Guinea Pig

The guinea pig is a very quick and simple pet to make.

Measurements
Length: 19cm (7½in)
Height: 5cm (2in)

Materials
Pair of 3¼mm (US 3) knitting needles
20g (¾oz) of Rowan Creative Focus Worsted in Golden Heather 018 (gh)
5g (⅛oz) of Rowan Wool Cotton in Tender 951 (te) for nose and paws
Tiny amount of Rowan Pure Wool DK Black 004 (bl) for eyes
Fishing line for whiskers

Abbreviations
See page 12.

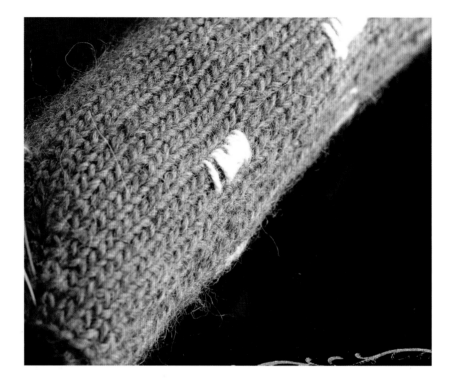

Body
With gh, cast on 36 sts.
Beg with a k row, work 2 rows st st.
Row 3: K11, k2tog, k10, k2tog, k11. *(34 sts)*
Row 4: Purl.
Work 4 rows st st.
Row 9: K16, k2tog, k16. *(33 sts)*
Work 43 rows st st.
Row 53: K8, k2tog, k2, k2tog, k5, k2tog, k2, k2tog, k8. *(29 sts)*
Row 54: Purl.
Row 55: K7, k2tog, k2, k2tog, k3, k2tog, k2, k2tog, k7. *(25 sts)*

FEET
The guinea pig's feet are embroidered on with pink yarn.

Row 56: Purl.
Row 57: K6, k2tog, k2, k2tog, k1, k2tog, k2, k2tog, k6. *(21 sts)*
Row 58: Purl.
Row 59: K5, k2tog, k7, k2tog, k5. *(19 sts)*
Row 60: Purl.
Cast (bind) off.

Ear

(make 2 the same)
With gh, cast on 2 sts.
Row 1: [Inc] twice. *(4 sts)*
Row 2: Purl.
Row 3: Inc, k2, inc. *(6 sts)*
Row 4: Purl.
Cast (bind) off.

To Make Up

SEWING IN ENDS Sew in ends, leaving ends from cast on and cast (bound) off rows for sewing up.
BODY With RS to RS, sew down bottom, then sew diagonally across top of bottom to form a curve. Sew along tummy and up the nose, leaving a 2.5cm (1in) gap in side for stuffing. Turn RS out.
STUFFING Stuff firmly, then sew up gap.
NOSE With te, embroider 5 parallel satin sts. Then with bl make 2 tiny diagonal stitches for nostrils and one vertical line from end of nose down 1cm (½in).
EYES With bl, make 4 satin stitches for each eye, pulling tightly through head to give characteristic sunken eyes.
EARS With RS facing forward, attach cast on row of ears to head with 6 sts between ears, approx 12 rows from nose.
PAWS With te, make 8 parallel rows of 5mm (¼in) satin stitches, 2 sts either side of centre seam, 22 and 38 rows back from nose.
WHISKERS Cut 3 x 8cm (3in) lengths of fishing line and thread through cheeks. Trim.

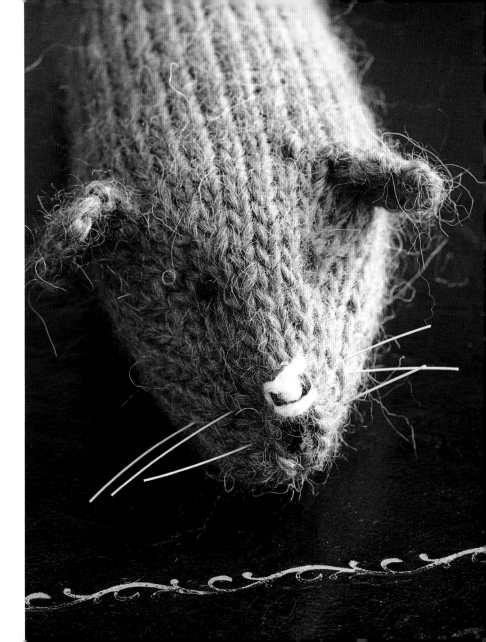

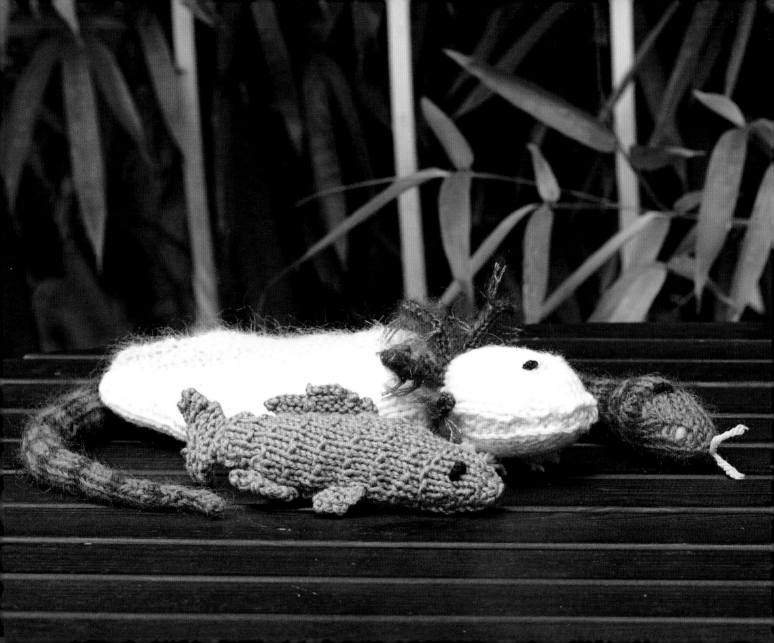

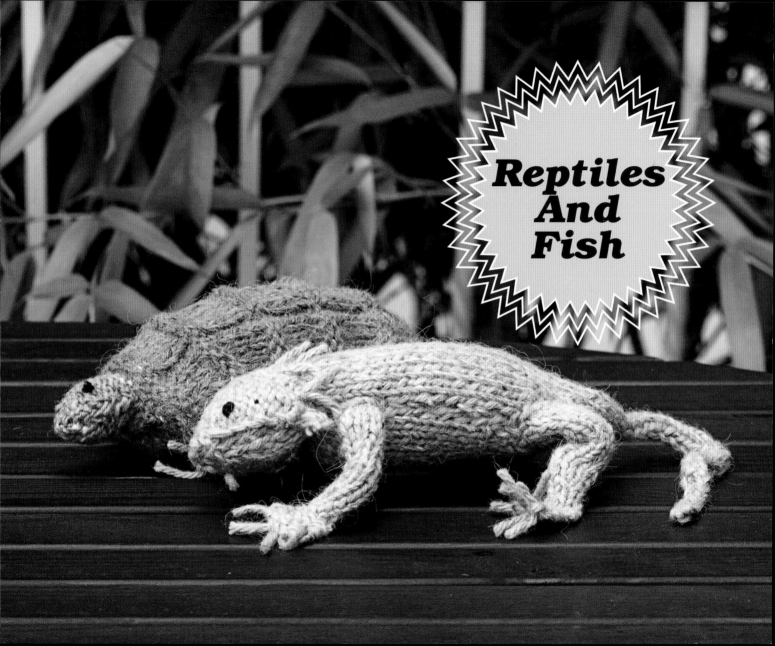

Reptiles
And
Fish

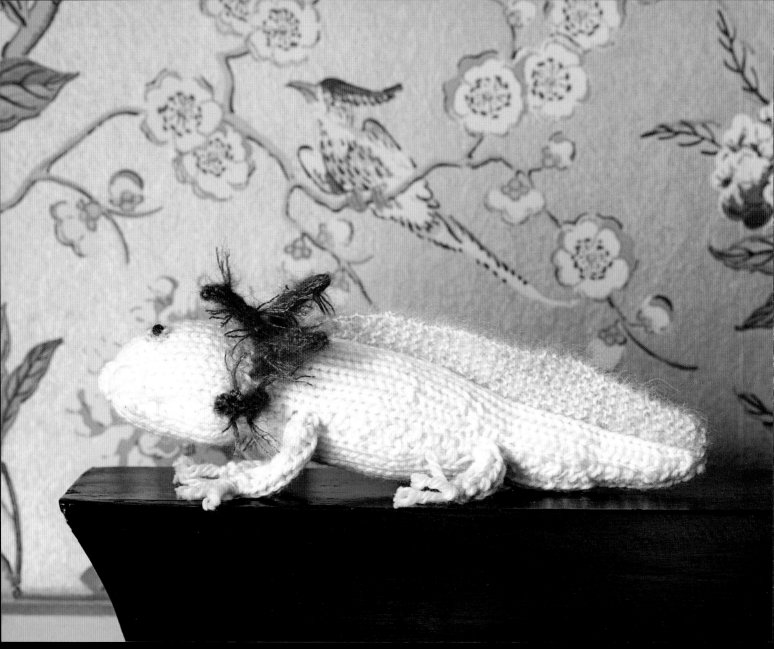

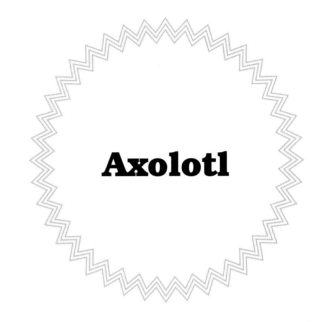

Axolotl

Forever the teenager, the axolotl is an amphibian closely related to the salamander. Ours is an almost transparent albino axolotl, but often they are varying shades of brown with spots.
An intriguing animal, they are endangered in the wild but have been successfully bred in captivity, becoming increasingly popular as pets.

Axolotl 🎗️🎗️

The details of the unique axolotl are important: the fins, claws and pronounced eyes.

Measurements
Length: 22cm (9in)
Height to top of head: 5cm (2in)

Materials
Pair of 3¾mm (US 5) knitting needles
Pair of 2¾mm (US 2) knitting needles (for back fin)
Crochet hook (for gills and claws)
15g (½oz) of Rowan Pure Wool Aran in Ivory 670 (iv)
5g (⅛oz) of Rowan Kidsilk Haze in Ghost 642 (gh) used DOUBLE throughout
5g (⅛oz) of Rowan Kidsilk Haze in Blushes 583 (bs) used DOUBLE throughout
2 pipecleaners for legs
Tiny amount of Rowan Pure Wool 4ply in Black 404 (bl) for eyes

Abbreviations
See page 12.
See page 13 for Scarf Fringe Method.

Back Legs
(make 2 the same)
With 3¾mm (US 5) needles and iv, cast on 5 sts.
Beg with a k row, work 6 rows st st.
Cast (bind) off.

Front Legs
(make 2 the same)
With 3¾mm (US 5) needles and iv, cast on 5 sts.
Beg with a k row, work 10 rows st st.
Cast (bind) off.

Body
(starting with the tail)
With 3¾mm (US 5) needles and iv, cast on 3 sts.
Beg with a k row, work 4 rows st st.
Row 5: Inc, k1, inc. *(5 sts)*
Work 7 rows st st.
Row 13: Inc, k3, inc. *(7 sts)*
Work 11 rows st st.
Row 25: K1, inc, k3, inc, k1. *(9 sts)*
Row 26: Purl.
Row 27: K2, inc, k3, inc, k2. *(11 sts)*
Work 5 rows st st.
Row 33: K2, inc, k5, inc, k2. *(13 sts)*
Work 13 rows st st.
Row 47: K3, k2tog, k3, k2tog, k3. *(11 sts)*
Row 48: Purl.
Row 49: K2tog, k1, k2tog, k1, k2tog, k1, k2tog. *(7 sts)*
Row 50: Purl.
Row 51: Inc, k1, inc, k1, inc, k1, inc. *(11 sts)*
Row 52: Purl.
Row 53: Inc, k2, inc, k3, inc, k2, inc. *(15 sts)*
Work 9 rows st st.
Row 63: K2tog, k2, k2tog, k3, k2tog, k2, k2tog. *(11 sts)*
Row 64: Purl.
Row 65: K1, k2tog, k5, k2tog, k1. *(9 sts)*
Row 66: P2tog, p5, p2tog. *(7 sts)*
Cast (bind) off.

Tummy
With 3¾mm (US 5) needles and iv, cast on 3 sts.
Beg with a k row, work 10 rows st st.
Row 11: Inc, k1, inc. *(5 sts)*
Work 19 rows st st.

Row 31: K1, inc, k1, inc, k1. *(7 sts)*
Work 17 rows st st.
Row 49: K2tog, k3, k2tog. *(5 sts)*
Row 50: Purl.
Row 51: K1, inc, k1, inc, k1. *(7 sts)*
Row 52: Purl.
Row 53: K1, inc, k3, inc, k1. *(9 sts)*
Work 9 rows st st.
Row 63: K2tog, k5, k2tog. *(7 sts)*
Row 64: Purl.
Row 65: K2tog, k3, k2tog. *(5 sts)*
Cast (bind) off.

Back Fin
With 2¾mm (US 2) needles and gh, cast on 4 sts.
Knit 10 rows.
Row 11: K1, inc, k2. *(5 sts)*
Knit 7 rows.
Row 19: K1, inc, k3. *(6 sts)*
Knit 29 rows.
Row 49: K1, k2tog, k3. *(5 sts)*
Knit 7 rows.
Row 57: K1, k2tog, k2. *(4 sts)*
Knit 5 rows.
Row 63: K1, k2tog, k1. *(3 sts)*
Knit 5 rows.
Row 69: K3tog and fasten off.

Gills
(make 6 in total)
With 2¾mm (US 2) needles and bs, cast on 4 sts.
For 2 gills: Beg with a k row, work 8 rows st st.
For 2 gills: Beg with a k row, work 10 rows st st.
For 2 gills: Beg with a k row, work 12 rows st st.
Cast (bind) off.

To Make Up
SEWING IN ENDS Sew in ends, leaving ends from cast on and cast (bound) off rows for sewing up.

LEGS With WS together, fold leg in half. Starting at foot, sew up leg on RS. Cut a pipecleaner to approximately fit length of leg, leaving an extra 2.5cm (1in) at both ends, then fold over 2.5cm (1in) of one end. With a little stuffing wrapped around it, push the folded end of the pipecleaner into leg. Leave top of leg open and an end of yarn to use for sewing leg to body.

BODY AND TUMMY With WS together and starting at the tail, sew the tummy to the body, leaving a 2.5cm (1in) gap in one side.

ATTACHING FIN Fold the body in half lengthways and starting at the tail and cast on row, attach the fin along the centre of the back, picking up a couple of bars between the sts on the body and following the line of the sts to keep the fin straight.

STUFFING Starting at the head, stuff the body then sew up the gap. Mould into shape.

ATTACHING LEGS Using the long end of yarn, attach the right front leg about 1cm (½in) from neck on the side seam, pushing the pipecleaner sticking out of the top of the leg into the body at the seam. Repeat for the left front leg. Attach the back legs at the end of the tail and beginning of the body as it increases, and sew on as for front legs.

GILLS Sew gills onto neck, starting with 8-row gill on the seam at neck, then leaving 1 st between each gill, sew on 10-row gill, then 12-row gill. Repeat for other side. Cut 16 x 5cm (2in) lengths of bs, and attach 4 tufts to each gill, 2 on each side, using the Scarf Fringe Method. Trim.

EYES With bl, sew 2-loop French knots positioned as in photograph. With gh, make a small loop around the French knot eye and sew it down using whip stitch, to encircle the eye.

CLAWS Cut 8 x 5cm (2in) lengths of iv, and with a crochet hook attach 2 tufts to base of each leg using the Scarf Fringe Method. Trim.

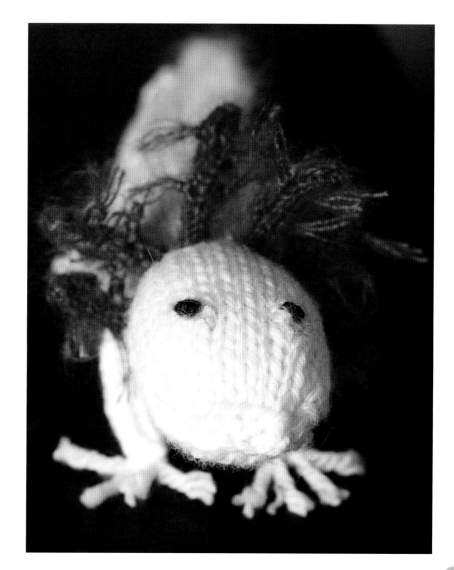

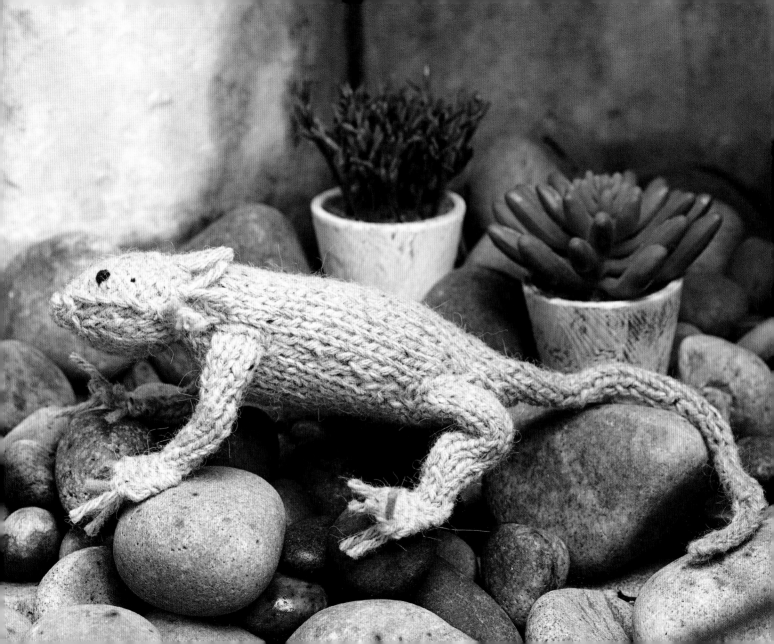

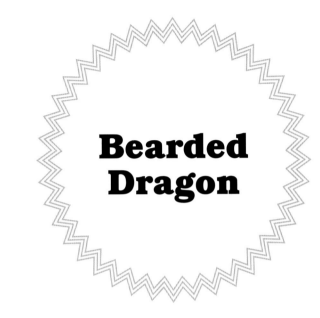

Bearded Dragon

Bearded dragons are not dragons, and they are not bearded, but they can puff out the skin on their neck and darken it to make it look like a beard. When a bearded dragon recognizes a member of its own species, it will stand on three legs and slowly wave one forelimb in a circular motion, a little like a member of our royal family. Daniel Gough's Bearded Dragon, Caspar, grew to an enormous size on a diet of crickets and not very much exercise.

Bearded Dragon

The Bearded Dragon has claws and a ruff made with tufts of yarn.

Measurements

Length (including tail): 35cm (13¾in)
Height: 5cm (2in)

Materials

Pair of 3¼mm (US 3) knitting needles
30g (1¼oz) of Felted Tweed Aran in Pebble 720 (pe)
3 pipecleaners for legs and tail
Crochet hook (for claws)
Tiny amount of Rowan Pure Wool 4ply in Black 404 (bl) for eyes

Abbreviations

See page 12.
See page 13 for Scarf Fringe Method.

Back Legs

(make 2 the same)
With pe, cast on 9 sts.
Beg with a k row, work 8 rows st st.
Row 9: K1, k2tog, k3, k2tog, k1. *(7 sts)*
Work 9 rows st st.
Row 19: K1, k2tog, k1, k2tog, k1. *(5 sts)*
Work 3 rows st st.
Work 6 rows garter st.
Cast (bind) off.

Front Legs

(make 2 the same)
With pe, cast on 7 sts.
Beg with a k row, work 6 rows st st.
Row 7: K1, k2tog, k1, k2tog, k1. *(5 sts)*
Work 11 rows st st.
Work 6 rows garter st.
Cast (bind) off.

Tail and Top of Body

With pe, cast on 2 sts.
Beg with a k row, work 14 rows st st.
Row 15: Inc, k1. *(3 sts)*
Work 9 rows st st.
Row 25: K1, inc, k1. *(4 sts)*
Work 15 rows st st.
Row 41: Inc, k2, inc. *(6 sts)*
Work 7 rows st st.
Row 49: Inc, k4, inc. *(8 sts)*
Work 3 rows st st.

Row 53: Inc, k6, inc. *(10 sts)*
Row 54: Purl.
Row 55: Inc, k8, inc. *(12 sts)*
Row 56: Purl.
Row 57: Inc, k10, inc. *(14 sts)*
Work 25 rows st st.
Row 83: K1, [k1, k2tog] 4 times, k1. *(10 sts)*
Row 84: P1, [p2tog] 4 times, p1. *(6 sts)*
Cont in rev st st to start head.
Row 85: Inc, p4, inc. *(8 sts)*
Row 86: Inc, k1, inc, k2, inc, k1, inc. *(12 sts)*
Row 87: Inc, p10, inc. *(14 sts)*
Work 5 rows st st.
Row 93: P1, p2tog, p1, p2tog, p2, p2tog, p1, p2tog, p1. *(10 sts)*
Row 94: Knit.
Row 95: [P1, p2tog] 3 times, p1. *(7 sts)*
Row 96: Knit.
Row 97: P3tog, p1, p3tog. *(3 sts)*
Row 98: K3tog and fasten off.

Underside

With pe, cast on 2 sts.
Beg with a k row, work 2 rows st st.
Row 3: [Inc] twice. *(4 sts)*
Row 4: Purl.
Row 5: Inc, k2, inc. *(6 sts)*
Work 7 rows st st.
Row 13: Inc, k4, inc. *(8 sts)*
Work 3 rows st st.
Row 17: Inc, k6, inc. *(10 sts)*
Row 18: Purl.
Row 19: Inc, k8, inc. *(12 sts)*
Work 27 rows st st.
Row 47: [K1, k2tog] 4 times. *(8 sts)*
Row 48: P1, [p2tog, p1] twice, p1. *(6 sts)*
Row 49: K2tog, k2, k2tog. *(4 sts)*
Row 50: P1, [inc purlwise] twice, p1. *(6 sts)*
Row 51: K1, inc into next 4 sts, k1. *(10 sts)*
Row 52: Inc, k8, inc. *(12 sts)*
Work 4 rows st st.
Row 57: K1, k2tog, k1, [k2tog] twice, k1, k2tog, k1. *(8 sts)*
Row 58: Purl.

Our bearded dragon is a lot cuddlier than the real thing.

Row 59: K1, [k2tog] 3 times, k1. *(5 sts)*
Row 60: Purl.
Row 61: K2tog, k1, k2tog. *(3 sts)*
Row 61: P3tog and fasten off.

To Make Up

SEWING IN ENDS Sew in ends, leaving ends from cast on and cast (bound) off rows for sewing up.

LEGS With WS together, sew up seam on outside, leaving 6 garter sts unsewn for foot. Cut a pipecleaner to fit approximately the length of both front legs, including where they pass through the body, leaving an extra 2.5cm (1in) at both ends, then fold over 2.5cm (1in) each end. With a little stuffing wrapped around, push the folded end of pipecleaner into each leg. Leave top of leg open and an end of yarn for sewing leg to body. Cut 12 x 4cm (1½in) lengths of pe, and with a crochet hook attach 3 tufts to each foot using the Scarf Fringe Method. Trim.

BODY Sew top of body to underside around head using whip stitch.

ATTACHING LEGS Using the long end of yarn, attach the front legs about 1cm (½in) from neck on the side seam. Attach the back legs in the same way, approx 7cm (2¾in) from front legs.

BODY CONT. Continue sewing down side of bearded dragon, leaving a 2.5cm (1in) gap in side. Attach top to underside across end of body.

STUFFING Starting at the head, stuff the body firmly, then sew up the gap.

TAIL Sew up tail with pipecleaner (with both ends folded over) inserted approx 7cm (2¾in) into tail and with approx 5cm (2in) sticking into body at tail end.

RUFF Cut 7 x 4cm (1½in) lengths of pe, and with a crochet hook attach tufts around where rev st st head meets body.

EYES With bl, sew 2-loop French knots positioned as in photograph.

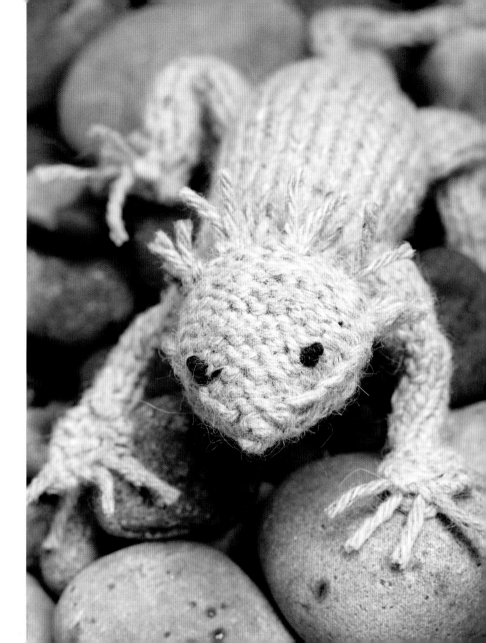

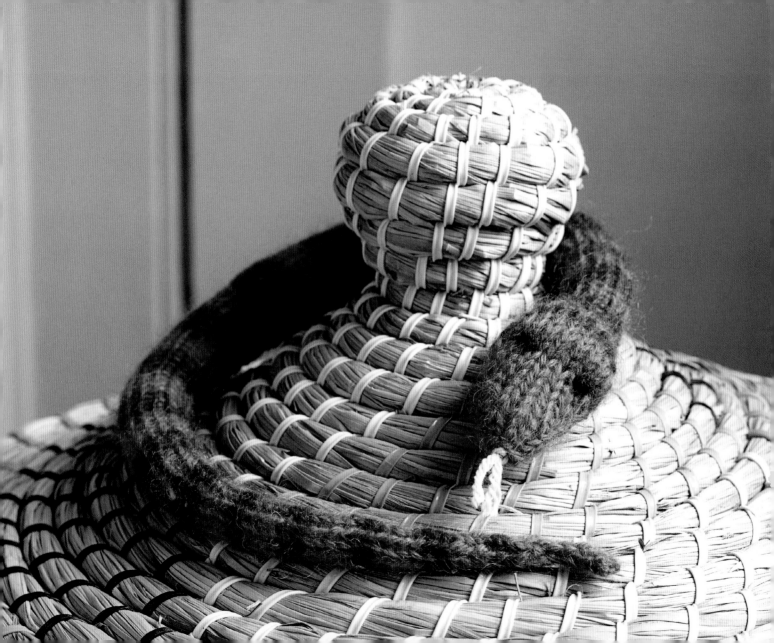

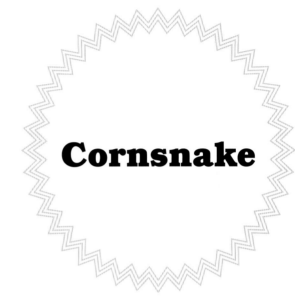

Cornsnake

A classic pet for the teenage boy, the cornsnake eats dead mice and live crickets. Although appearing self-contained, a friend of mine's snake escaped from its vivarium only to be found three months later on the front door step. Perhaps a snake is more attached than we imagine?

Cornsnake

Very easy to make, even
easier if knitted in one
colour, without stripes.

Measurements
Length: 50cm (20in)
Height to top of head: 3cm (1¼in)

Materials
Pair of 3¾mm (US 5) knitting needles
10g (¼oz) of Rowan Kid Classic in Rosewood
870 (rd)
10g (¼oz) of Rowan Kid Classic in Earth 872
(ea)
Tiny amount of Rowan Pure Wool 4ply in
Black 404 (bl) for eyes
Tiny amount of Rowan Pure Wool 4ply in
Shell 468 (sh) for tongue
Crochet hook for tongue

Abbreviations
See page 12.
See page 13 for Scarf Fringe Method.

**Why not knit more
rows to make the
cornsnake longer?**

Body
With rd, cast on 3 sts.
Beg with a k row, work 6 rows st st.
Row 7: Inc, k1, inc. *(5 sts)*
Row 8: Purl.
Change to ea (do not cut off rd yarn, hold at
side of work).
Work 2 rows st st.
Change to rd (do not cut off ea yarn, hold at
side of work).
Work 4 rows st st.
Change to ea.
Work 2 rows st st.
Change to rd.
Work 4 rows st st.
Change to ea.
Work 2 rows st st.
Change to rd.
Row 23: Inc, k3, inc. *(7 sts)*
Work 3 rows st st.
Change to ea.
Work 2 rows st st.
Change to rd.
Work 4 rows st st.
Rep last 6 rows once more.
Change to ea.
Work 4 rows st st.
Change to rd.

Row 43: Inc, k5, inc. *(9 sts)*
Work 3 rows st st.
Change to ea.
Work 4 rows st st.
Change to rd.
Work 4 rows st st.
Rep last 8 rows twice more.
Change to ea.
Work 4 rows st st.
Change to rd.
Row 75: Inc, k7, inc. *(11 sts)*
Work 3 rows st st.
Change to ea.
Work 6 rows st st.
Change to rd.
Work 4 rows st st.
Rep last 10 rows twice more.
Change to ea.
Row 109: K2tog, k7, k2tog. *(9 sts)*
Work 5 rows st st.
Change to rd.
Work 2 rows st st.
Change to ea.
Work 4 rows st st.
Change to rd.
Row 121: K2tog, k5, k2tog. *(7 sts)*
Row 122: Purl.
Change to ea.
Work 4 rows st st.
Change to rd.
Work 2 rows st st.
Change to ea.
Work 4 rows st st.
Change to rd.
Row 133: K2, inc, k1, inc, k2. *(9 sts)*
Row 134: P2, inc, p3, inc, p2. *(11 sts)*
Change to ea.
Row 135: K2, inc, k5, inc, k2. *(13 sts)*
Row 136: P3, inc, p5, inc, p3. *(15 sts)*
Change to rd.
Row 137: K3, inc, k7, inc, k3. *(17 sts)*
Row 138: P4, inc, p7, inc, p4. *(19 sts)*
Change to ea.
Work 2 rows st st.

Change to rd.

Row 141: K4, k2tog, k7, k2tog, k4. *(17 sts)*
Row 142: P3, p2tog, p7, p2tog, p3. *(15 sts)*
Row 143: K3, k2tog, k5, k2tog, k3. *(13 sts)*
Row 144: P2, p2tog, p5, p2tog, p2. *(11 sts)*
Row 145: K2, k2tog, k3, k2tog, k2. *(9 sts)*
Row 146: Purl.
Row 147: K2, k2tog, k1, k2tog, k2. *(7 sts)*
Row 148: Purl.
Cast (bind) off.

To Make Up

SEWING IN ENDS Sew in ends, leaving ends from cast on and cast (bound) off rows for sewing up.
BODY AND STUFFING With WS together and using one of the two colours, start at tail and sew short section of body together. Stuff that section, then sew up a bit more of body and stuff, until whole snake is stuffed and head is sewn up. Mould body into shape.
EYES With bl, sew 3-loop French knots positioned as in photograph.
TONGUE Cut a 2.5cm (1in) length of sh. Use crochet hook and scarf fringe method to attach tongue to tip of head.

EYES
The eyes are French knots, but you could use black beads.

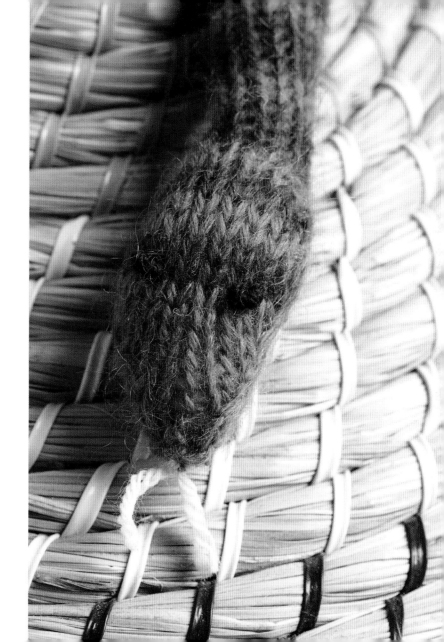

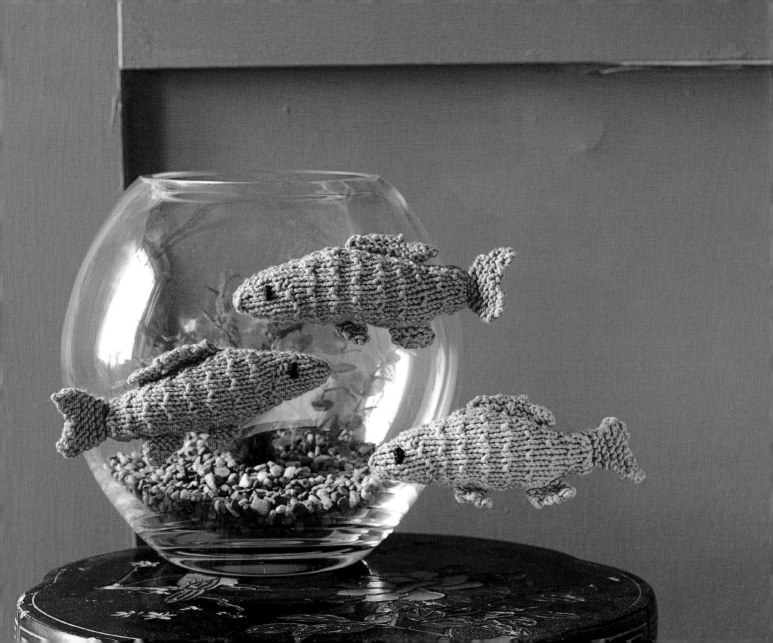

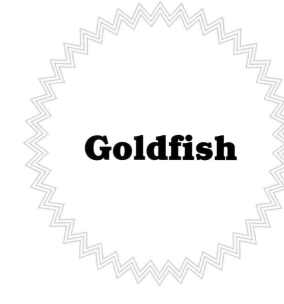

Goldfish

Often a child's first pet, the goldfish is a freshwater fish and member of the carp family. A clever fish, after a few weeks, he will no longer consider you to be a threat and will even take food from your hand. A goldfish used to be a popular prize at fairgrounds; fortunately this is no longer the case. Magicians used to perform a popular 'swallowing the goldfish' trick, fooling many; it was in fact a piece of carrot.

Goldfish

Try knitting a shoal of gold and orange goldfish.

Measurements
Length: 15cm (6in)
Height to top of head: 4cm (1½in)

Materials
Pair of 2¾mm (US 2) knitting needles
Double-pointed 2¾mm (US 2) knitting needles (for holding stitches)
10g (¼oz) of Rowan Wool Cotton in Café 985 (ce) or Brolly 980 (by)
Tiny amount of Rowan Pure Wool 4ply in Black 404 (bl) for eyes

Abbreviations
See page 12.

Bottom Half of Tail Fin
With ce, cast on 2 sts.
Row 1: Knit.
Row 2: K1, inc. *(3 sts)*
Row 3: Inc, k2. *(4 sts)*
Row 4: K3, inc, (break yarn and hold sts on a spare needle). *(5 sts)*

Top Half of Tail Fin and Right Side of Body
With ce, cast on 2 sts.
Row 1: Knit.
Row 2: Inc, k1. *(3 sts)*
Row 3: K2, inc. *(4 sts)*
Row 4: Inc, k3. *(5 sts)*
Work two halves of tail fin together as folls:
Row 5: K5 from Top Half and k5 from spare needle of Bottom Half. *(10 sts)*

Row 6: K2tog, k6, k2tog. *(8 sts)*
Knit 2 rows.
Row 9: K2tog, k4, k2tog. *(6 sts)*
Knit 2 rows.
Row 12: K2tog, k2, k2tog. *(4 sts)*
Knit 2 rows.
Right side of body
Row 15: Inc, k2, inc. *(6 sts)*
Row 16: Purl.
Row 17: [K1, p1] 3 times.
Beg with a p row, work 3 rows st st.
Row 21: [P1, k1] 3 times.
Row 22: Purl.
Row 23: Inc, k4, inc. *(8 sts)*
Row 24: Purl.
Row 25: [P1, k1] 4 times.
Row 26: Purl.
Row 27: K7, inc. *(9 sts)*
Row 28: Purl.
Row 29: [K1, p1] 4 times, k1.
Row 30: Purl.
Row 31: K8, inc. *(10 sts)*
Row 32: Purl.
Row 33: [P1, k1] 5 times.
Row 34: Purl.
Row 35: K9, inc. *(11 sts)*
Row 36: Purl.
Row 37: [K1, p1] 5 times, k1.
Work 3 rows st st.
Row 41: [P1, k1] 5 times, p1.
Row 42: Purl.
Row 43: K2tog, k7, k2tog. *(9 sts)*
Row 44: Purl.
Row 45: [P1, k1] 4 times, p1.
Row 46: Purl.
Row 47: K2tog, k5, k2tog. *(7 sts)*
Row 48: P4, k3.
Row 49: K3, p1, k3.
Row 50: P2, k1, p4.
Row 51: K4, p1, k2.
Row 52: Purl.
Row 53: K2tog, k3, k2tog. *(5 sts)*
Work 3 rows st st.
Row 57: K2tog, k1, k2tog. *(3 sts)*

Row 58: Purl.
Cast (bind) off.

Left Side of Body
With ce, pick up without knitting 4 sts from row 14 on tail, starting at bottom edge of the bottom side of fish.
Row 1: Inc, k2, inc. *(6 sts)*
Row 2: Purl.
Row 3: [K1, p1] 3 times.
Beg with a p row, work 3 rows st st.
Row 7: [P1, k1] 3 times.
Row 8: Purl.
Row 9: Inc, k4, inc. *(8 sts)*
Row 10: Purl.
Row 11: [P1, k1] 4 times.
Row 12: Purl.
Row 13: Inc, k7. *(9 sts)*
Row 14: Purl.
Row 15: [P1, k1] 4 times, p1.
Row 16: Purl.
Row 17: Inc, k8. *(10 sts)*
Row 18: Purl.
Row 19: [P1, k1] 5 times.
Row 20: Purl.
Row 21: Inc, k9. *(11 sts)*
Row 22: Purl.
Row 23: [P1, k1] 5 times, p1.
Work 3 rows st st.
Row 27: [K1, p1] 5 times, k1.
Row 28: Purl.
Row 29: K2tog, k7, k2tog. *(9 sts)*
Row 30: Purl.
Row 31: [K1, p1] 4 times, k1.
Row 32: Purl.
Row 33: K2tog, k5, k2tog. *(7 sts)*
Row 34: K3, p4.
Row 35: K3, p1, k3.
Row 36: P4, k1, p2.
Row 37: K2, p1, k4.
Row 38: Purl.
Row 39: K2tog, k3, k2tog. *(5 sts)*
Work 3 rows st st.
Row 43: K2tog, k1, k2tog. *(3 sts)*

Row 44: Purl.
Cast (bind) off.

Top Fin
With ce, cast on 12 sts.
Row 1: Inc, k9, k2tog. *(12 sts)*
Row 2: K2tog, k9, inc. *(12 sts)*
Row 3: Cast (bind) off 5 sts, k5 icos, k2tog.
(6 sts)
Row 4: K2tog, k4. *(5 sts)*
Cast (bind) off.

Front Bottom Fin
With ce, cast on 5 sts.
Row 1: Knit.
Row 2: K2tog, k3. *(4 sts)*
Row 3: K2, k2tog. *(3 sts)*
Row 4: K2tog, k1. *(2 sts)*
Row 5: K2tog and fasten off.

Back Bottom Fin
With ce, cast on 6 sts.
Knit 2 rows.
Row 3: K2tog, k4. *(5 sts)*
Row 4: K3, k2tog. *(4 sts)*
Row 5: K2tog, k2. *(3 sts)*
Row 6: K1, k2tog. *(2 sts)*
Row 7: K2tog and fasten off.

To Make Up
SEWING IN ENDS Sew in ends, leaving ends from cast on and cast (bound) off rows for sewing up.
BODY With WS together, sew around body and head, leaving a 2.5cm (1in) gap in the middle of the body.
STUFFING Starting at the head, lightly stuff the goldfish, then sew up the gap.
FINS Sew cast on row of top fin onto top of the body. Sew cast on row of bottom fins, leaving 2cm (¾in) between the two fins, onto bottom of body.
EYES With bl, sew 3-loop French knots positioned as in the photograph.

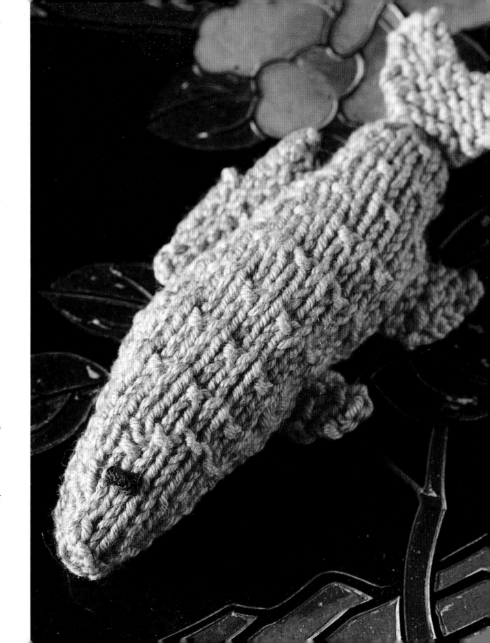

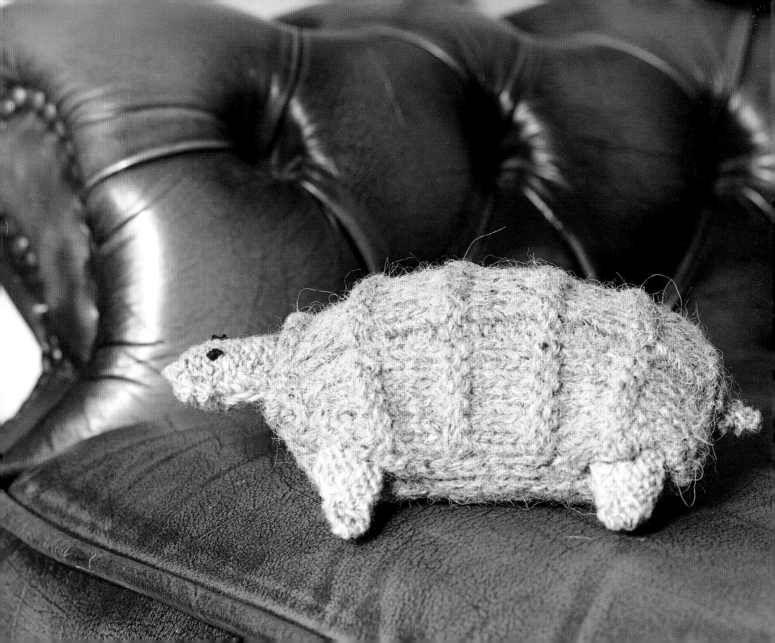

Tortoise

Tortoises have been on Earth for more than 200 million years. The difference between a tortoise and a turtle is that turtles live in water, whereas tortoises live on land. The oldest Giant Tortoise in the world was caught at approximately 50 years old and went on to live for another 152 years. When holding a tortoise it's best to put a hand underneath its body, as tortoises become stressed if they feel air beneath them. The tortoise in Aesop's fable *The Tortoise and the Hare* won the race by dogged determination, a lesson for us all.

Tortoise 🎗🎗

The tortoise wears his shell like a tank top.

Measurements
Length: 20cm (8in)
Height: 7cm (2¾in)

Materials
Pair of 3¼mm (US 3) knitting needles
25g (1oz) of Rowan Felted Tweed Aran in Cork 721 (co)
15g (½oz) of Rowan Tweed in Bedale 581 (be)
Tiny amount of Rowan Pure Wool 4ply in Black 404 (bl) for eyes

Abbreviations
See page 12.

Shell
With co, cast on 16 sts.
Beg with a k row work 2 rows rev st st.
Row 3: Inc, p2, k2, p6, k2, p2, inc. *(18 sts)*
Row 4 (RS): K4, p2, k6, p2, k4.
Row 5: Inc, p3, k2, p6, k2, p3, inc. *(20 sts)*
Row 6: K5, p2, k6, p2, k5.
Row 7: Inc, p4, k2, p6, k2, p4, inc. *(22 sts)*
Row 8: K6, p2, k6, p2, k6.
Row 9: Inc, k20, inc. *(24 sts)*
Row 10: Purl.
Row 11: Inc, p6, k2, p6, k2, p6, inc. *(26 sts)*
Row 12: P2, k6, p2, k6, p2, k6, p2.
Row 13: K2, p6, k2, p6, k2, p6, k2.
Rep rows 12-13 once more.
Row 16: As row 12.
Beg with a k row, work 2 rows rev st st.
Row 19: K2, p6, k2, p6, k2, p6, k2.
Row 20: P2, k6, p2, k6, p2, k6, p2.

Rep rows 19-20 twice more.
Beg with a k row work 2 rows rev st st. *Row 26 completed*
Rep rows 19-26 once more.
Row 35: K2tog, p6, k2, p6, k2, p6, k2tog. *(24 sts)*
Row 36: P2tog, k5, p2, k6, p2, k5, p2tog. *(22 sts)*
Row 37: P6, k2, p6, k2, p6.
Row 38: K6, p2, k6, p2, k6.
Row 39: P6, k2, p6, k2, p6.
Row 40: K6, p2, k6, p2, k6.
Row 41: Knit.
Row 42: Knit.
Row 43: K2tog, k5, cast (bind) off 8 sts, k5 icos, k2tog. *(6 sts either side of gap)*
Row 44: K2tog, k4, cast on 8 sts, k4, k2tog. *(18 sts)*
Row 45: Purl.
Beg with a k row, work 4 rows st st.
Row 50: Inc, k16, inc. *(20 sts)*
Beg with a p row, work 23 rows st st.
Row 74: K2tog, k16, k2tog. *(18 sts)*
Row 75: Purl.
Row 76: K2tog, k14, k2tog. *(16 sts)*
Row 77: Purl.
Row 78: K2tog, k12, k2tog. *(14 sts)*
Row 79: Purl.
Row 80: K2tog, k10, k2tog. *(12 sts)*
Row 81: Purl.
Cast (bind) off.

Body
(make 2 the same)
With be, cast on 1 st.
Row 1 Inc. *(2 sts)*
Row 2: Knit.
Row 3: [Inc] twice. *(4 sts)*
Row 4: Knit.
Row 5: Knit.
Row 6: Knit.
Row 7: Inc, k2, inc. *(6 sts)*
Row 8: Knit.
Row 9: Inc, k4, inc. *(8 sts)*
Row 10: K8, cast on 6 sts. *(14 sts)*
Row 11: P14, cast on 6 sts. *(20 sts)*
Row 12: K20, cast on 8 sts. *(28 sts)*
Row 13: P28, cast on 8 sts. *(36 sts)*
Row 14: K2tog, k32, k2tog. *(34 sts)*
Row 15: P2tog, p30, p2tog. *(32 sts)*
Row 16: K2tog, k28, k2tog. *(30 sts)*
Row 17: P2tog, p26, p2tog. *(28 sts)*
Row 18: Cast (bind) off 5 sts, k21 icos, k2tog. *(22 sts)*
Row 19: Cast (bind) off 5 sts, p to end. (17 sts)
Work 18 rows st st.
Row 38: K17, cast on 8 sts. *(25 sts)*
Row 39: P25, cast on 8 sts. *(33 sts)*

Make your tortoise into a turtle by giving him longer flippers instead of feet.

Row 40: K2tog, k29, k2tog. *(31 sts)*
Row 41: P2tog, p27, p2tog. *(29 sts)*
Row 42: K2tog, k25, k2tog. *(27 sts)*
Row 43: P2tog, p23, p2tog. *(25 sts)*
Row 44: Cast (bind) off 10sts, k to end. *(15 sts)*
Row 45: Cast (bind) off 10sts, p5 to end. *(5 sts)*
Work 4 rows st st.
Row 50: Inc, k3, inc. *(7 sts)*
Work 5 rows st st.
Row 56: Inc, k5, inc. *(9 sts)*
Row 57: Purl.
Row 58: K2tog, k5, k2tog. *(7 sts)*
Row 59: P2tog, p3, p2tog. *(5 sts)*
Row 60: K2tog, k1, k2tog. *(3 sts)*
Row 61: P3tog and fasten off.

To Make Up

SEWING IN ENDS Sew in ends, leaving ends from cast on row and cast (bound) off rows for sewing up.

BODY With knit sides together sew up sides of tortoise on outside leaving a 2.5cm (1in) gap in side. Stuff firmly, slipping extra stuffing into top to give the shell a hump, then sew up gap.

SHELL With WS together sew 3 sts across shoulders either side of head. Sew 2.5cm (1in) down either side, leave gap of 4cm (1½in) for front legs, sew 5cm (2 in), leave another 4cm (1½in) gap for back legs. Put tortoise body inside shell before sewing up second side in same way.

Pull head, legs and tail through holes.

EYES With bl make 3-loop French knots for eyes, approx 6 rows back from nose.

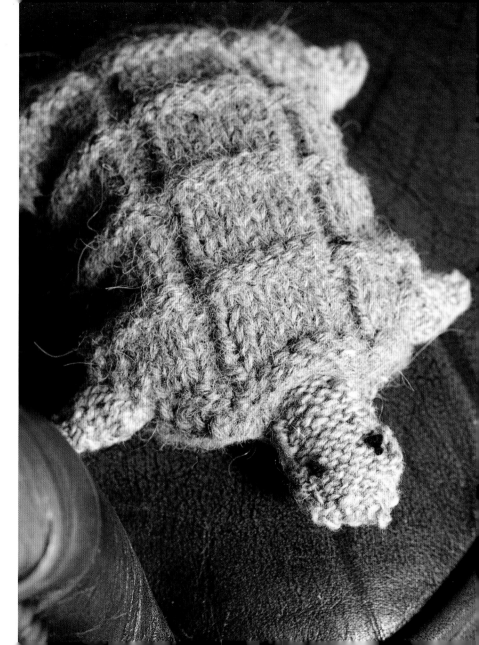

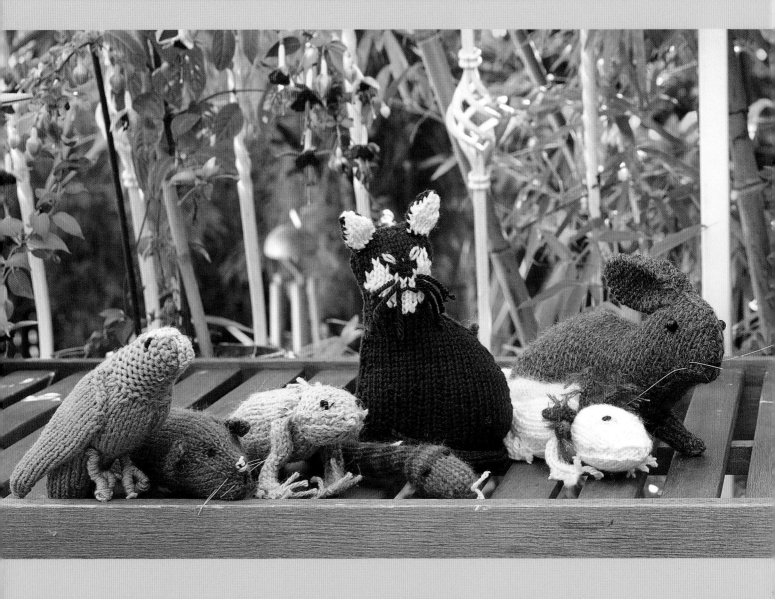

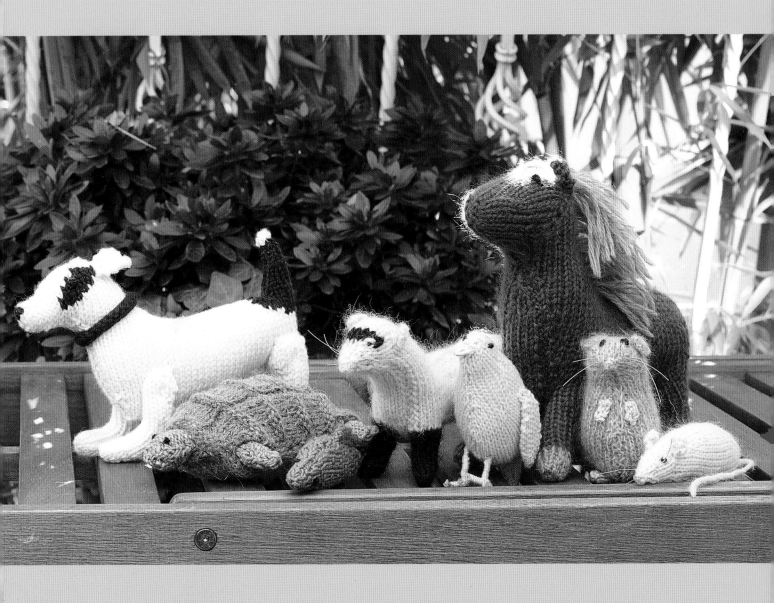

Index of Pets

Small And Furry

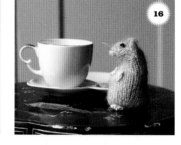

16

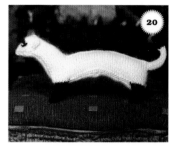

20

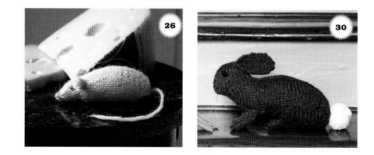

26

30

Birds

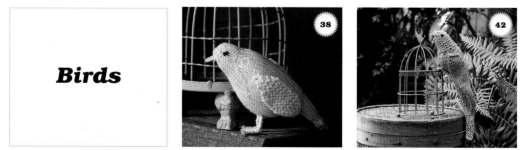

38

42

Four-Legged Friends

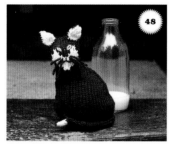

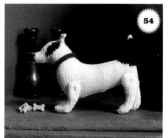

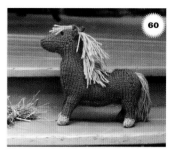

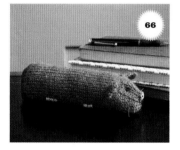

Reptiles And Fish

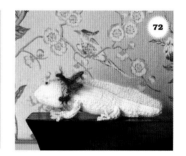

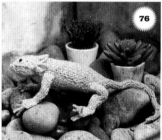

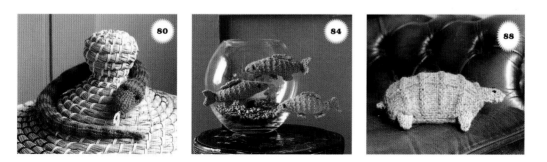

Resources

All the animals are knitted in Rowan Yarns; for stockists please refer to the Rowan website: www.knitrowan.com.
By the time this book is printed some colours may have been discontinued, but John Lewis department stores stock Rowan, and will happily suggest alternative colours.
We recommend using 100 per cent polyester or kapok stuffing, available from craft shops and online retailers. A pet takes 15g–40g (½–1½oz) of stuffing, depending on size.
We are selling knitting kits for some of the pets. The kits are packaged in a *Best In Show* knitting bag and contain yarn, all needles required, stuffing, pipecleaners and a pattern.
For those who cannot knit but would like a pet, we are selling some of the pets ready-made. You can see the pets on our website: www.muirandosborne.co.uk.

The Authors

Sally Muir and Joanna Osborne run their own knitwear business, Muir and Osborne. They export their knitwear to stores in the United States, Japan and Europe as well as selling to shops in the United Kingdom. Several pieces of their knitwear are in the permanent collection at the Victoria and Albert Museum, London.

They are the authors of the bestselling *Best in Show: Knit Your Own Dog, Best in Show: 25 More Dogs to Knit, Best in Show: Knit Your Own Cat,* and *Knit Your Own Zoo.*

Acknowledgements

We have been lucky enough to work with the same group of people for this book, So, at the risk of sounding repetitive... thank you so much to Katie Cowan and Amy Christian for sticking with us, to Laura Russell for her excellent design work, Marilyn Wilson for her eagle-eyed pattern checking, and Kate Haxell for being Queen of Knitting. Thank you yet again to Holly Jolliffe for a brilliant job with the photography and taking time off from the gorgeous Frida to do it. And to Caroline Dawnay and Sophie Scard for all the work they have done on our behalf. Thank you yet again to Rowan for being so generous with the yarns.

Join our online community at
www.bestinshowbooks.com

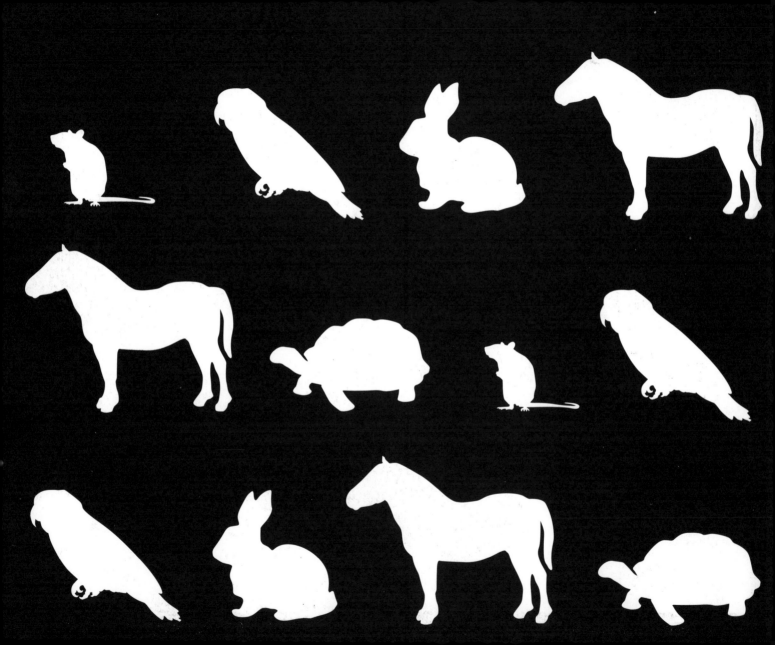